WHAT PEOPLE ARE SAYING ABOUT SAM CHAND...

Sam Chand has dedicated his life to champion the success of others. Known as a "dream releaser," Sam is a leader of leaders who will constantly challenge and lift our mind-sets, self-imposed limitations, and unexamined choices. Sam writes from the enormous wealth of his own experience with uncanny insight, good humor, and pragmatic advice.

—*Brian Houston*
Global Senior Pastor, Hillsong Church

Sam Chand's teaching is a secret weapon resulting in the increase of effective materialization of your unrealized potential.

—*Bishop T. D. Jakes*
New York Times Best-Selling Author

Chand has been one of the most valuable mentors in my life and ministry. He has tremendous character, valuable leadership insight, a contagious sense of humor, and a pastor's heart. He has mentored me and made me a much stronger spiritual leader.

—*Craig Groeschel*
Senior Pastor, Life.Church

Samuel Chand is a leader's leader. His keen insights and vast leadership exposure have prepared him well for resourcing the kingdom. His natural passion for leadership development is a refined gift he enthusiastically shares with leaders and developing leaders.

—*John C. Maxwell*
Founder, EQUIP
New York Times Best-Selling Author

No one does this better than Sam Chand and I can say that from our experience working with him in my own church. His reputation for helping companies find their way in the twenty-first century is exemplary and his integrity is beyond reproach.

—*Jentezen Franklin*
Senior Pastor, Free Chapel
New York Times Best-Selling Author

Great leaders have mastered the art of asking great questions, but legendary leaders like Sam Chand have mastered the art of questioning their own thinking.

—*Steven Furtick*
Founder and Lead Pastor, Elevation Church

Change is on the horizon, but it will not come by accident—it will require intentionality by those who lead the way! As a voice of influence on the subject of leadership, my friend Sam Chand will help you shape your future by reshaping the way you think!

—*John Bevere*
Best-Selling Author and Minister
Cofounder, Messenger International

One of the most respected voices on church and ministry leadership today is Sam Chand. On his website, his tag line is, "My life's vision is helping others succeed"—and he's good at it. Sam and I have shared a number of clients over the years, and time and time again, I've seen him turn around struggling churches, inspire frustrated leaders, and transform the culture at failing organizations.

—*Phil Cooke*
Media Producer and Consultant
Author, *The Way Back*

Just when I thought my friend Sam Chand had reached his pinnacle, he transcends to a new dimension. Sam has a masterful skill of asking piercing questions, which are better questions that lead to better answers and ultimately a better life!

—*Bishop Dale C. Bronner*
Author/Founder, Word of Faith Family Worship Cathedral

Sam Chand will expand your thinking, give you fresh tools, and help you navigate your leadership journey.

—*Mark Batterson*
Lead Pastor, National Community Church

HARNESSING THE

POWER

OF

TENSION

HARNESSING THE
POWER
OF
TENSION

STRETCHED BUT NOT *BRO*KEN

SAMUEL R. CHAND

W
WHITAKER
HOUSE

HARNESSING THE POWER OF TENSION
Stretched but Not Broken

Samuel R. Chand Consulting
950 Eagle's Landing Parkway Suite 295 ♦ Stockbridge, GA 30281
www.samchand.com

ISBN: 978-1-64123-497-9 ♦ eBook ISBN: 978-1-64123-498-6

Printed in the United States of America
© 2020 by Samuel R. Chand
All rights reserved.

Whitaker House
1030 Hunt Valley Circle ♦ New Kensington, PA 15068
www.whitakerhouse.com

Library of Congress Cataloging-in-Publication Data
Names: Chand, Samuel, 1952- author.
Title: Harnessing the power of tension : stretched but not broken / Samuel R. Chand.
Description: New Kensington, PA : Whitaker House, [2020] | Summary: "Examines the idea that tension is not a flaw, a threat, or a problem, but a reality of life that is inevitable and, in many cases, desirable when used confidently and creatively"— Provided by publisher.
Identifiers: LCCN 2020026507 (print) | LCCN 2020026508 (ebook) | ISBN 9781641234979 (hardcover) | ISBN 9781641234986 (ebook)
Subjects: LCSH: Stress (Psychology)
Classification: LCC BF575.S75 C435 2020 (print) | LCC BF575.S75 (ebook) | DDC 155.9/042—dc23
LC record available at https://lccn.loc.gov/2020026507
LC ebook record available at https://lccn.loc.gov/2020026508

1 2 3 4 5 6 7 8 9 10 11 **WJ** 27 26 25 24 23 22 21 20

CONTENTS

1

TENSIONS IN YOUR PERSONAL LIFE

Some tension is necessary for the soul to grow, and we can put
that tension to good use. We can look for every opportunity to
give and receive love, to appreciate nature, to heal our wounds
and the wounds of others, to forgive, and to serve.
—Joan Borysenko, Ph.D.[1]

The word *tension* comes from the Latin word *tendere*, which means "to
stretch." It's not a bad thing to be stretched in our careers, our parenting,
our ministries, or our leadership. When we aren't stretched, we become

stagnant and stop growing. We might even say that tension is both *inevitable* and, at least in many cases, *desirable* in life and leadership.

Brenda and I got married in Atlanta in 1979, and we soon moved to Gresham, Oregon, a suburb of Portland. Both of us got jobs; in addition, I served as the youth pastor of a church. The next year, we heard about a church that was looking for a senior pastor—it was Brenda's home church in Hartford, Michigan, where her parents still lived. I was definitely interested in the position. I applied, but strangely, I didn't get a reply.

The recent history of the church had been anything but smooth sailing. The previous pastor had been *voted out*, which means he was fired. This kind of situation virtually always causes people to take sides, for or against the pastor, and the animosity can split a church. The final straw happened at a congregational vote in April of that year; that's when they took the deciding vote. The church was exhausted by conflict by the time Brenda and I arrived in July for our vacation to visit her parents. That Sunday, Brenda and I showed up at the church, and a couple of the leaders asked me if I would preach. I was excited! This could be my opportunity to fulfill my dream and become a pastor! I don't know if I impressed them or if they were simply too desperate to turn me down, but I asked them to make a decision the day I preached, and they did: I was in. However, I soon learned that I wasn't the first choice of the church leaders or the people. In fact, I was their last choice, but no one else would take the position.

Brenda and I went back to Oregon to pack up and move to the little town in Michigan. In my first service in August, I counted thirteen people, including Brenda and me. Without us, the "congregation" (it was more like a small group) was in single digits.

The church leaders said they could only pay me $125 a week, but we could live in the parsonage that was attached to the church building. Our living room shared a wall with the baptistery. When we arrived, Brenda was in her eighth month of pregnancy with our first child. We were embarking on several new adventures at the same time.

In a rural setting, churches grow when the pastor makes personal visits to homes to get to know people, pray with them, eat their cookies, taste their homemade jam, and invite them to church. I left home early each morning and traveled around a wide area to visit people who came to church, those who might come to church, and those who had never thought about coming to church. I got home late every night and started over again the next morning. It was especially important for me to make these visits on Friday and Saturday because then people couldn't use the excuse of "I forgot" and miss church the next day or so.

My efforts paid off. The congregation quickly grew to thirty, then fifty, then eighty, and then a hundred. Each Sunday, we saw more cars in the parking lot, people were getting saved, and the offering grew. I was utterly exhausted, but I was thrilled that the church was growing so much so fast.

During all of this, however, Brenda was at home—very pregnant and very alone. This was before the days of cell phones and even before pagers. The only way we could stay in touch during the day was to put quarters into payphones—and I had precious few quarters. We had scheduled the delivery at a hospital in St. Joseph, a town about twenty miles away. If Brenda needed me, there was no way to contact me when I was visiting people in their homes.

For a while, she tried to be tough, but before too long, I came home to the sounds of her crying. She was afraid the baby would come and no one would be there to take her to the hospital. With the utmost sensitivity, I told her, "Just call your parents. They live only three miles away and they can get here very quickly." I paused a second and then gave her one more instruction: "But before you walk out, leave me a note."

For some strange reason, my solution didn't cause Brenda to feel understood and cherished. I had read in *Reader's Digest* that pregnant women go through hormonal changes as their delivery date nears, so I chalked her tears up to that.

On the first Saturday in October in 1980, I came home late at night. This time, Brenda wasn't crying. I wasn't sure if that was good or bad.

I soon found out. As soon as I walked in the door, she said, "I need to talk to you."

That statement always has ominous implications for any husband. It's never, "You're such a great husband! I appreciate you so much!"

I sat down near her. She looked at me and said plainly, "Sam, everyone in the church has a pastor...except me." She paused for a second and then told me, "I'm scared. I'm having my first baby. I'm lonely and I have a lot of pain. I need a pastor, so I'm going to start going to another church, starting tomorrow."

Obviously, she had been thinking about this for a while—she named the church *and* the pastor of that church.

Instantly, my mental wheels began to whirl. I pictured Brenda driving out of our parking lot at the same time other people were driving in. In a small town, everyone knows everybody's business, and the news that a pastor's wife was going to a different church would spread like wildfire. Most importantly, from my point of view, my credibility would be crushed.

Over a long and sleepless night, I wrestled with God. I told Him, "This doesn't make sense. I'm working like crazy and the church is growing, but my marriage is crumbling. How can it happen that You're blessing me in my work for the church, but things at home are bleak and dark?" I was confused and desperate. I thought I was doing exactly what God had called me to do, but my home life was a train wreck. Wasn't I seeking first the kingdom of God and letting Him add all things to my life? I wasn't sinning and the church was doing well. What was I missing?

At some point in the middle of the night, I sensed the Lord say to me, "What does it profit Sam if he gains the whole church but loses his wife?" The next morning, I apologized to Brenda and assured her that I was going to change. She must have believed me because she didn't go to the other church. Today, we've been married over four decades. Our lives have been very busy, but we've found a way to make each other a priority. (I'm quite sure I've had far more adjustments than Brenda has!)

This tension point was, in some ways, completely predictable. We were young and idealistic. I had a new job and I wanted to succeed in it. Brenda was having our first child. We had very little money. I had achieved my highest goal of being a pastor and I loved what I was doing. We had been married only a year, and before we could make the normal adjustments, a truckload of new challenges came our way. We had relocated across the country twice in the first fourteen months of our marriage.

I wish I could say that I experienced a dramatic turning point that night, and that it's all been great since then…but it wouldn't be the truth. The changes happened slowly, incrementally, with a number of fits and starts. One Sunday a few days after I realized I had better be a pastor to Brenda too, we were standing at the front of the church after the service, shaking hands and speaking to everyone who had come. A lady named Charlene stepped up to me and grabbed my lapels. She looked me in the eyes and said, "Listen to me, boy. Take care of your wife."

I instantly felt insulted. *Why did she feel she had to be so blunt? Why was she being so disrespectful and mean? Why did she call me "boy"?* But days later, I realized that Charlene loved me more than almost anyone else in the church. Somehow, she looked past its growth and saw what was going on in our marriage. And that day, she spoke truth to me.

Someone once asked me when I resolved the tension between work and family, and I answered, "Not yet." To be honest, I'm still on the journey to understand Brenda and live with the tension of two hearts, two personalities, two different backgrounds, and two people pursuing a single purpose together.

I want to examine this tension more fully, as well as explore others that exist in our personal lives.

FAMILY AND WORK

When we experience pressure at work and tension at home, we feel we have nowhere to go where we can relax. When we're at work, we're preoccupied with an argument we had with our spouse or kids; when we're at home, we can't stop thinking about the deadline we're afraid we're going to miss, or the boss's stinging criticism. Obviously, we can't focus on only one of these priorities.

Home is supposed to be *a city of refuge* where we feel safe, understood, and supported. We have to work to make a living, but we want our home life to be happy. When both spouses are in the workforce, the tension points multiply. We need guardrails to protect our home environment from the work pressures that can consume us.

One of the most common complaints of couples is that they talk past each other when they try to communicate at a deeper level. Typically, when women talk about what's bothering them, they want to feel heard and understood, but the man feels compelled to fix the problem—often with a quick answer that implies, "Why haven't you thought of this?" When she feels put down, he responds, "I was just trying to help you!" When more tension is applied from any source—like struggles with money, kids, and in-laws—these gender tendencies become even more pronounced and the division grows.

When men share their struggles, they usually want the women in their lives to affirm their manhood by saying something like, "Wow, you really work hard! I can't believe you put up with so much at work to provide for our family!" He doesn't want her to step in with three simple steps to fix the problem.

> **WHEN MORE TENSION IS APPLIED FROM ANY SOURCE, GENDER TENDENCIES BECOME EVEN MORE PRONOUNCED AND THE DIVISION GROWS.**

The communication of the struggle may sound the same, but each one wants something different. In many (but not all) cases, she's looking for tenderness and empathy, while he's looking for respect and affirmation.

These misunderstandings can happen on any topic, but they're perhaps most common when people share their struggles at work. Work-life balance has been a popular concept for many years and the principles related to it are gradually becoming more sophisticated. In an article for *Forbes*, Alan Kohll observes what the pursuit of balance looks like for different generations. To summarize his findings:

+ Baby Boomers (born between 1945 and 1960) had parents who lived through the Depression and World War II. Boomers longed for the stability of a steady job and enough income. Their high commitment to their careers caused them to forfeit a sense of balance, so they report high levels of tension.

+ Gen X (born between 1961 and 1980) experienced the stress caused by their parents' dedication to work, and they reacted to the imbalance. For them, the pendulum swung the other direction to prioritize their families over their careers. They value flexibility in their work schedule, telecommuting, and plenty of time for vacations.

+ Millennials (born between 1981 and 2000) often have been misunderstood by employers. These young people shoulder enormous student loan debt, face soaring housing prices, and don't mind changing jobs if they find something else that looks more attractive. Employers have tried for years to attract and keep them by providing an array of perks at the office, but many Millennials say these things aren't important to them. More than half report they are worried about finding a meaningful career. Kohll concludes:

Creating a flexible work environment is one of the best ways to satisfy the work-life balance needs of most employees—no matter which generation they belong to.... It's important for employers to realize that work-life balance is about more than just hours. Besides promoting flexibility, employers should also strive to improve the overall workplace experience for their employees. Prioritizing a healthy culture and cultivating a happy workplace environment promotes work-life balance. When employees are happy in their roles, work will feel more like a second home, and less like working for a paycheck. Employers should prioritize competitive compensation, comfortable office conditions, opportunities for professional growth and opportunities for social connections.[2]

+ Generation Z (born after 2000) value flexibility and meaning at work as much as a good salary. They want—and expect—communication with their employers and supervisors. Feedback isn't a luxury; it's a necessity. They may have grown up in the digital age, but they thrive on human interaction.[3]

The tension between work and home isn't one we can completely resolve. We can look for companies that value flexibility and create a healthy culture, and we can learn to communicate with our spouse and children in ways that promote understanding and support, but the tension will always be with us.

> WE MAKE A MISTAKE WHEN WE TRY TO MICROMANAGE OUR SCHEDULES TO GIVE EACH SIDE EQUAL TIME AND ATTENTION. EQUAL TIME DOESN'T NECESSARILY MEAN EQUAL VALUE.

We make a mistake when we try to micromanage our schedules to give each side equal time and attention. Equal time doesn't necessarily mean equal value. It's more reasonable to step back a bit, recognize seasons and special circumstances, and build healthy rhythms into our lives. For instance, young mothers don't have time for a lot of relaxation and reflective reading, people who are involved in moving from one community to another are consumed with the myriad of details—and couples with newborns who are moving barely have time to breathe! There's no need to feel guilty during these and similar situations that require more of us, but at the right time, we can adjust our priorities. A common problem is that some people fail to make this adjustment. The frantic pace during a particularly stressful season of life becomes the new normal. It's wise to recognize the seasons, look for special circumstances, make the necessary adjustments, and create healthy rhythms.

THEM AND ME

Some of us have devoted our lives to help others grow, but too often, we do little if anything to promote our own development. We need to invest in our own sanity, joy, and talents. In Stephen Covey's popular book, *The 7 Habits of Highly Effective People*, the last habit is to "sharpen the saw." This means we invest in ourselves in four areas:

+ Physical

+ Social/emotional

+ Mental

+ Spiritual

Covey gives this advice: "You have to decide what your highest priorities are and have the courage—pleasantly, smilingly, nonapologetically—to say 'no' to other things. And the way you do that is by having a bigger 'yes' burning inside. The enemy of the 'best' is often the 'good.'"[4] Investing in these four areas is a "best" practice for all of us.

We may experience seasons when we're giving out far more than we're taking in. When I was a new pastor, I prepared four messages every week, for Sunday morning, Sunday night, a young adult leadership class, and Wednesday night Bible study. My lifestyle was really no different from a teacher, a plumber, a mom, or an attorney. All of us pour ourselves out for others. The question for us is simple but stark: Is more going out of our emotional and intellectual tanks than is going in? If it is, we'll soon be running on empty, with all the corollary results of impatience, discouragement, a hair trigger on our emotions, and an undercurrent of resentment.

What fills your tank on a regular basis? It may be time with friends, exercise, reading books that aren't related to your profession, eating a nice dinner with someone you love, playing with your kids or grandkids, golfing, fishing, or any other endeavor that recharges your batteries. If we wait too long between fill-ups, we'll almost certainly need even more resources to fill our tanks. Don't wait. Develop the habit of regularly filling your tank. Yes, you have responsibilities. Yes, there are demands on your time and energy. And yes, you have to give a lot at home and at work, but if your tank runs dry, you won't have *anything* to give.

THE QUESTION FOR US IS SIMPLE BUT STARK: IS MORE GOING OUT OF OUR EMOTIONAL AND INTELLECTUAL TANKS THAN IS GOING IN?

Some will argue, "But Jesus gave everything to the point of death." Yes, but if we look at the rhythms of His life, we'll see that Jesus often got away from the busyness of His ministry to spend time in prayer, relax with His closest followers, and enjoy connecting with others in the homes of friends. Few of us are called to die for our faith, but all of us are called to live a vibrant, passion-filled, purposeful life for God. We can't do that if we're exhausted, angry, and hopeless.

This principle isn't only true for us. One of the ways we give to others is to help them create space to regularly recharge their batteries. All of us need a blend of relaxation and stimulation to keep our bodies, minds, and hearts running well. I've used the analogies of filling a tank and recharging a battery. Another one is a bank account: if our withdrawals exceed our deposits, we may survive for a while, but sooner or later, we'll be emotionally, physically, and relationally bankrupt. Don't let that happen to you!

SUCCESS AND FULFILLMENT

We might be tempted to use these words as synonyms, but actually, they're in tension with one another. Success is visible achievement and is usually measured in power, popularity, positions, and possessions; fulfillment is the intangible sense that we're living for a higher purpose, that our lives count, and that we're making a difference in the lives of others. There *is* a difference, but we need to avoid the mistake of making them polar opposites.

There's nothing wrong with success. Achieving tangible goals gives us a sense of accomplishment. But this feeling is only temporary. If pastors see more people coming into church, they always want more. When business leaders see their companies grow, they always strive for more sales, more market share. Far too often, when we reach a milestone, we're thrilled for a while (sometimes a very short while) until we look around and see someone who has a little more power, or people who have friends who are a bit cooler than ours, nicer things, and a title on the office door that's a step or two above ours.

We can use success to fulfill our purpose, but too often, the trappings of success become more important than our purpose—and in fact, we might become so consumed in our pursuit of the tangible that we lose track of the intangible. When we become obsessed with the next measure of success, tension multiplies, we use people instead of loving them, and we suffer from the full range of stress-related problems.

> **WHEN WE BECOME OBSESSED WITH THE NEXT MEASURE OF SUCCESS, TENSION MULTIPLIES, WE USE PEOPLE, AND WE SUFFER FROM A RANGE OF STRESS-RELATED PROBLEMS.**

Best-selling author John Ortberg identifies this tension by describing our *mission* (fulfillment) and our *shadow mission* (valuing success over our true, God-given purpose). Actually, the more talented and successful we are, the more we're tempted to live for our shadow mission.

Ortberg writes:

Part of what makes the shadow mission so tempting is that it's usually so closely related to our gifts and passions. It's not

180 degrees off track; it is just 10 degrees off track, but that 10 degrees is in the direction of hell.... If we fail to embrace our true mission, we will live out our shadow mission. We will let our lives center around things that are unworthy, selfish and dark.[5]

The problem Ortberg describes is the failure to live in the tension— we give ourselves wholeheartedly to the visible trappings of success without using them to fulfill our true purpose. This is not a rare phenomenon. Virtually every advertisement and most conversations assume that the highest goals in life are the elements of success. In an article about this tension, Dr. Theresa Bullard comments:

> While attaining external markers of success can be a great thing, having them as the main goal and driver ignores our deeper purpose and desires. When we feel unfulfilled, unworthy, unloved, a sense of lack or "not enough", then the pattern tends to be to try and fill that void with "success" and "things." In some cases such success can actually take us away from our fulfillment due to distraction and pursuing the wrong things. This is literally the opposite of fulfillment!
>
> Fixating on succeeding can cause major stress about producing a result or from overworking. Stress is known to affect health, well-being, and even lead to depression, addictions, and a life out of balance, which overall lowers the quality of life.[6]

God graciously gives us many things to enjoy. These things give us delight and satisfaction, and the proper response is to realize their source and thank God for His kindness and generosity. But if these things become our central goal, our primary pursuit, we'll be driven instead of thankful, fearful of not measuring up instead of resting in the goodness of God, and looking over our shoulders to compare our success with others instead of delighting in all God has given us.

In this life, we're a mixed bag. We won't have pure motives until we see Jesus face to face, but in the meantime, we can be aware that the visible can overwhelm the invisible. Gradually, we can learn to live in the tension between outward success and inward fulfillment, and we can experience increasing levels of gratitude and passion. We need to muster the courage to at least ask why we drive a particular kind of car, why we live in the house we bought, why we wear particular clothes, and why we post what we do on social media. The answers may challenge us to realize the important tension between success and fulfillment.

Fulfillment is about relationships. We enjoy a sense of fulfillment when our kids or grandkids jump in our laps and tug on our ears. We have a vicarious fulfillment when our children's marriages and careers are going well. A parent's level of happiness often coincides with that of their most unhappy child.

> **MY DEEPEST SENSE THAT MY LIFE'S MISSION IS BEING FULFILLED IS WHEN I'M MEETING WITH ONE PERSON.**

I'm invited to speak at some of the greatest churches in the world. It's an honor to be there and it certainly is a measure of success to be accepted so warmly. But my level of fulfillment is inversely proportional to the size of the audience. My deepest sense that my life's mission is being fulfilled is when I'm meeting with one person to talk about what's most meaningful to him or her.

WHO WE ARE AND WHO GOD WANTS US TO BE

In a way, we're *double exposures*. The Scriptures tell us that we're loved, forgiven, and accepted by the grace of God...but we still sin. In fact, we're so sinful that it took the death of the Son of God to pay for our sins. He still loves us and values us more than the stars in the sky. Whatever your finely tuned biblical anthropology may be, we can all admit that we haven't yet arrived. Even the apostle Paul came to that conclusion. He was one of the most gifted leaders in all of history, but he knew there was more: he was still striving, still pressing, still leaning in to know, love, and serve Jesus more fully. He wrote to the Philippians about his steadfast commitment. After listing his many accomplishments and his high status in the Jewish community, he turned all of this on its head. He explained that his status and his accomplishments no longer meant anything to him. The only thing that mattered was experiencing the love of Jesus. (See Philippians 3.) But Paul was realistic about the Christian life being a process—often a long, slow process—of transformation. He wrote the people in the church that he wasn't satisfied with his spiritual growth. He was still leaning hard into God's love and His purposes for him.

This wasn't a new thought in his letter. In his opening remarks, he reminded the Christians in Philippi that someday, their transformation would be complete—not today and not tomorrow, but someday when we see Jesus face to face. God gives us a thirst for Him and for meaning, and it's our goal to pursue Him with all our hearts to let Him quench this thirst, but we realize it won't be fully quenched until we arrive in the new heavens and new earth. For now, there's always more.

I live in this tension. I'm very grateful for all God has done in me, for me, and through me, but I'm still reaching for more. Why am I writing this book? Because there are more concepts for me to share. Why do I travel to speak and consult? Because God has given me a purpose and a calling. Why do all of us carve out time to pray, study the Bible, serve those in need, love our families and friends, and worship with other believers? Because we're on a journey to discover more of the wonders of who God is and who He has created us to be.

THE GIFT AND THE GIFTS

All of us have multiple gifts, talents, and abilities; we also have one or two that are more significant than the others. The tension is to give enough focus to the *primary* gift so we aren't distracted by the *many* gifts. For instance, I do a lot of things—writing, speaking, leading, and consulting—but my greatest impact is spending quality time with a leader.

I've seen people settle for being generalists instead of investing resources to become excellent at their primary talent, so they don't function in their *sweet spot*. Others are tremendously gifted in an area, but they're already in a job that's comfortable and making money doing something else. It's important to maximize our best talent. How do we identify and sharpen our biggest, God-given gift? Let me give you three principles:

ALL OF US HAVE MULTIPLE GIFTS, TALENTS, AND ABILITIES. THE TENSION IS TO GIVE ENOUGH FOCUS TO OUR PRIMARY GIFT SO WE AREN'T DISTRACTED BY THE REST.

1. Your gift has to be *discovered.*

Who has told you, "You know, you're really good at..."? What are the activities that bring you the most joy, that energize you, that fill your emotional tank? What are the things you naturally gravitate toward? What does your heart dwell on in your downtime? The answers to these questions will probably give you an open window to see your primary gift.

2. Your gift has to be *developed.*

Even the most gifted athletes spend countless hours honing their skills, and the best musicians practice incessantly. You're no different. To sharpen your talent, you need to invest in training, mentoring, and finding opportunities to practice. Sometimes, these require a significant outlay of money and the investment of a lot of time, but quite often, you're so eager to excel in this area that you don't mind at all.

3. Your gift has to be *deployed.*

Practice must have a purpose; talent needs to be activated. You need to find ways to use your gift, even sporadically, so you can sharpen your skills and get some exposure to find new opportunities. Over time, you'll discover where you're most successful and fulfilled. In the process, you may uncover a gift that has been dormant for many years…or perhaps never noticed until that moment. Sooner or later, you have a decision to make: you can either stay in your current role but tailor your job responsibilities around your gift, or you can find a new role that maximizes your talents.

When we identify and begin to excel in our primary gift, we face other tensions. For instance, our passion may not readily provide a job with a steady income. Plenty of waiters and waitresses are making a living while they look for opportunities to do something they hope to do. They live in the *in between* for a while as they make a living and look for a chance to do something they really love.

> **YOU CAN EITHER TAILOR YOUR CURRENT JOB RESPONSIBILITIES AROUND YOUR GIFT, OR YOU CAN FIND A NEW ROLE THAT MAXIMIZES YOUR TALENTS.**

When we're afraid of the tensions in our personal lives, we'll either ignore them, drift to one of the extremes to find quick answers, or crater under the strain of not knowing how to live in them. But if we embrace these tensions, we can step back to see them more clearly, understand the complexities, find rhythms that work for us, and trust God to lead us to more love and fulfillment than we ever dreamed possible.

THE COMPLEXITY OF TENSION

Some of us are very concrete: we assume we can segment every area of our lives so we can address the challenges and take advantage of the opportunities in each one. The persistent presence of tension in one area, however, bleeds over and affects other parts of our lives. In other words, the breakfast menu isn't two separate eggs sunny side up; they're thoroughly scrambled! Tensions at work affect how we treat people at home, tensions at home consume our thoughts so we aren't as sharp at work, and tensions related to health concerns, financial setbacks, strained relationships, an empty nest, aging parents, and the full range of possible stress points affect other areas of our lives, no matter how hard we try to put them in their own boxes.

Of course, greater and more prolonged tension has a much larger impact. Living with significant tension over a long period of time erodes the body's ability to cope, the mind's capacity to think, and our emotional potential to bounce back. We need insight to see how tension is affecting us and we need courage to take action to resolve what we can. We're fooling ourselves, though, when we assume one area of our lives doesn't affect the others.

MY HOPE FOR YOU

As you read this book, I hope you'll realize that the presence of tension isn't a flaw in you or a threat from others. It's not a problem to solve, but a strain to be used. When you develop this perspective and you encounter tension, you'll be less confused, you'll feel less guilty because you understand that the tension isn't the result of your error or flaw, and you'll experience less pressure to figure everything out and less compulsion to resolve it quickly and completely.

As you internalize the principles in these chapters, you won't be surprised when people have commitments, even passionate commitments, to their points of view. You'll learn to affirm them, listen to them, and use their energy to find workable solutions.

AS YOU BECOME MORE CONFIDENT IN USING TENSION CREATIVELY, YOU WON'T MAKE ASSUMPTIONS AND YOU WON'T BE BULLIED.

As you become more confident in using tension creatively, you won't jump to make assumptions about a person's motives, you won't be bullied when they demand their way, you won't overlook them when they try to hide, and you'll see through their efforts to reduce the tension by appeasing others.

When we accept tension as a reality of life, we gain confidence and mental clarity when we encounter it. We become wiser and more approachable. Our focus isn't on getting rid of tension, but using it to create something better than before. We don't walk on eggshells, afraid to say the wrong thing. We learn when to speak up, when to ask questions, when to listen, and when to let things go.

If we believe that if we're good people we won't have any tension, we'll create a kind of tension that can eat us alive. I've heard it said that, "Your happiness is inversely proportional to your shoulds." A corollary is, "More shoulds, less joy." I think that's absolutely true. As we relax in the middle of tension, we see people and situations more clearly, and we invite our families and teams into the process of creatively using tension in life and leadership.

At the end of each chapter, you'll find some reflection questions and an application exercise. Don't rush through these. Take your time: think, pray, and write. You can also use these to stimulate discussion on teams and in groups.

THINK ABOUT IT:

1. Have you experienced a lack of balance between your family and work? If so, how did it affect you and your most important relationships?

2. How would it help you to establish rhythms in finding the right blend of time with your family and work? What might those rhythms look like?

3. In the past year, how would you describe your *tank*, your *battery*, or your *bank balance?* How much is going in and how much is going out? Does anything need to change? If so, what steps do you need to take?

4. How would you describe the differences between success and fulfillment? Why do you think success is often more attractive than fulfillment?

5. If we're *double exposures*, what are some insights that can keep us from being discouraged that we aren't making more progress in our spiritual lives?

6. As you look back on the last few years, how have you seen your gift come to life? What can you do to develop it and deploy it?

APPLY IT:

- As you read this chapter, what tensions described here reminded you of your experiences?

- How did you respond at the time?

- How do you want to respond next time?

- Who do you know who is experiencing a similar tension today?

- How can you help this person embrace the tension, resolve the tension, or use the tension to stimulate an innovative solution?

2

TENSIONS WITH PEOPLE

Life is a series of pulls back and forth....
A tension of opposites, like a pull on a rubber band.
And most of us live somewhere in the middle....
Which side wins? Love wins. Love always wins.
—Mitch Albom[7]

A few years ago, the CEO of a large organization called and asked me to fly in to meet with him. He explained that he wanted me to help him with the direction for their future, "and oh yeah, some staff issues."

When we met, I asked him to tell me what was going on. Over the next ninety minutes, he told story after story about tensions he was under. In all the stories, I heard the same name:

> When *this* happened, Charlie did *this*, "and it caused a lot of problems...." When *that* happened, "Charlie jumped in and made a mess of things.... Charlie came to me with this complaint.... When I cast a vision for our company, Charlie spoke up and tried to shoot it down.... Charlie started this program and it cost far more than he budgeted for it.... I've been told that there's an underground resistance movement in the company and I hear that Charlie is leading it...."

And on and on and on.

During our meeting, the future direction of the organization wasn't mentioned, and there weren't generic *staff issues*—there was only the *Charlie issue.* The CEO's leadership and life were consumed by his relationship with Charlie. In fact, he measured every decision by how he thought Charlie would respond. Charlie was a division leader, but in effect, he was running the company. He had become a rock in the CEO's shoe, a constant and painful nuisance.

As I've met with hundreds if not thousands of leaders in businesses, churches, and nonprofits, I've noticed one constant: there's always *a Charlie.* There's always someone on a team, committee, or board who exercises disproportional power and control.

Similarly, I've met with many presidents, CEOs, board chairmen, and pastors who have told me that in their top leadership meetings of, say, five people, four of them are engaged, perceptive, flexible, future-oriented, hopeful, and positive, but one always has a *"but...."* This person—we'll call her Susie—is much like Charlie: negative, pessimistic, distracting, and draining, usually while smiling and appearing to be a team player.

The rest of the people are eager to debate concepts and procedures. They're looking for a positive outcome. But Susie just wants to control the meeting and wield power by throwing up objections. Often, she communicates with emotion to force people to back down. She may not win the argument, but she bullies people enough to stop the team from making progress. She blurts out, "We can't do that! It's dumb!" "That'll never work!" "We've tried that before. It didn't work then and it won't work now!"

I'm sure you're thinking of your own Charlie or Susie right now!

When the leader of the organization is preparing for this meeting, he's primarily thinking about Susie, the *but...* person, and he tailors his presentation to placate her. When the leader is riding on the elevator or driving to the meeting, he's thinking about Susie again, wondering how he can say just the right thing in just the right way to get her to agree with the new plans. During the leader's presentation as he casts vision, suggests steps forward, and leads the discussion, he's paying far more attention to Susie than all of the others. And several times during the meeting, he refers back, "As Susie said earlier..." He's patronizing her with the hope of winning her positive influence.

Susie lives in the leader's head. She occupies prime real estate. The leader lives to please her, or at least to limit the damage she can cause, but appeasement is the worst way to lead.

The leader may not be aware of what has happened, but his grand vision for the organization has been whittled down, mashed, and limited by his anticipation of how one negative person will respond. Everything revolves around the one person who has the least passion, the smallest vision, and the most cynicism of anyone on the leadership team. Of course, Susie assumes she's playing a vital role by bringing *realism* to the team, but everyone knows pessimism isn't realism.

Why doesn't the leader confront her? Oh, he has—many times, in fact, but always with suggestions, never with clear expectations and consequences. Outside observers have every reason to wonder if it's even possible for the leader of a large and prestigious organization to let this go on and on.

Yes, it's possible. In fact, it happens all the time.

The same dynamic happens in family interactions at most holiday dinners and family gatherings. There's always somebody, maybe *"crazy Aunt Sally,"* who everyone is thinking about as they plan the event, during it, and long after it. Some people may not even come if she's going to be there, some may leave in a huff because she has offended them 453 times (they've been keeping track) and they're not going to take it anymore. And everybody talks about Aunt Sally for the next few days.

> **TO THE DEGREE OUR CONNECTIONS WITH PEOPLE ARE LIFE-GIVING, WE THRIVE; TO THE EXTENT THEY DRAIN US OR HARM US, WE WILT.**

We need loving, trusting relationships like we need water, food, and air. To the degree our connections with people are life-giving, we thrive; to the extent they drain us or harm us, we wilt. Even the best relationships, though, include their share of tension. We need to understand the normal tensions so we can build healthy relationships.

LEADING AND BEING LED

We might think that the people whose names are on the top of the organizational chart aren't being led by anyone...but that's not the case. All of us, no matter what position we hold, are accountable to someone: a boss, a board, shareholders, or a mentor. Of course, most of us are somewhere else on the organizational chart besides the top slot, and it's easy to see who we're leading and who's leading us. The fact that we're leading while being led produces a number of tensions:

1. We have authority, but we have to submit to those who hold us accountable.

2. We're leaders, but we lead best by serving.

3. We value creativity and innovation, but certain things have to get done... and done on time.

4. We have a vision for the future, but so do those holding us accountable, and their vision may be different than ours.

5. We push for growth but we always need to consolidate the gains.

THE DISCIPLES' TENSION

We see this tension played out in Jesus's relationship with the disciples. Matthew tells us, *"Jesus called his twelve disciples together and gave them authority to cast out evil spirits and to heal every kind of disease and illness"* (Matthew 10:1 NLT). I can imagine them responding, "Fantastic! That's what I'm talking about!" But soon after this, in the same chapter, Jesus warned them, *"If you cling to your life, you will lose it; but if you give up your life for me, you will find it"* (Matthew 10:39 NLT). Those who follow Jesus have been given authority, but they give up *their* authority… at the same time.

All authority is delegated or borrowed authority. We don't invent it or manufacture it. Someone above us gives us responsibility, resources, and a role. If we arrogantly claim authority comes from us, we'll abuse it and use it to dominate others. But if we accept it from the hand of another, we can wield it with humility and strength.

In my years of meeting with leaders in the corporate and church worlds, I've heard a number of statements that are at least yellow flags, if not red ones, that tell me about a person's perception of authority. Here are a few:

"I serve the vision, not the leader. I really don't respect him at all."

"Do what you want in the organization—except for my area. Leave me and my area alone!"

"I hate to say it, but I'm a much better leader than my boss (or pastor)."

"Nobody around here works as hard as I do."

"My leader would be a lot better off if he'd follow my advice."

Do you hear echoes of conversations you've had or overheard over the years? Or have any of these comments come out of your mouth? They reveal that the person insists on being a leader but resents being led.

To lead well while we're being led, let me offer a few recommendations. I've adapted these from my friend Chris Sonksen, the founder and leader of a church growth organization called Boom:

1. Develop an ownership spirit. That is, take responsibility without complaining or blaming.

2. Manage the organization's money as if it were your own.

3. Honor your leader, even when you disagree with a policy, and honor the people who report to you, treating them the way you'd want to be treated in their position.

4. Develop the ability to see what your leader sees. As you walk around, notice the spot on the carpet, the sticking door, the receptionist who's grouchy. Don't wait for the leader to notice them and take action. Do what you can to fix these problems.

5. Speak your leader's language. Observe what inspires her and what discourages her.

6. Create margin in your leader's life by doing your job so well that he never has to worry about you and never has to chase you down to remind you to do something you've been assigned. Don't be a sycophant, but find ways to encourage your leader.

7. Keep developing your skills and your capacity. Invest in yourself by getting a mentor or coach, reading books and journals in your area, listening to podcasts, and watching videos by leaders in your field. Do you think you don't have time for these things? Look hard at your schedule and find the time.

8. Learn to ask great questions. I've noticed that people who excel in their jobs have the ability to ask penetrating questions that get to the heart of people and uncover the complexity of systems and processes.

9. Never violate trust. Speak the truth, don't participate in gossip, resolve disputes with the person without letting resentment fester, be on time, and use your authority to build people up.

10. Communicate clearly, often, and well. Don't assume people understand because you've said something once. Develop the reflex of asking, "Tell me what you heard me say."[8]

All of us—from CEOs to every line on the organizational chart and people in every family—live in the tension of leading while being led. We don't have the ultimate power to do whatever we want to do; we're not in complete control. And yet we've been given authority to take responsibility in our organizations and our homes, to be submissive to those over us and lead people with strength and grace.

INFLUENCE AND INFLUENCERS

We can have a certain amount of influence ourselves, but we have far deeper and wider impact if we multiply ourselves by recruiting, training, equipping, and placing others to have influence. One of the most significant trends in online marketing is the hiring of social media influencers. These people are paid to tell the world what they think of products and others flock to their sites.

In an article on this subject, Carla Rivera explains:

A social media influencer is a user who has established credibility in a specific industry, has access to a huge audience and can persuade others to act based on their recommendations. An influencer has the tools and authenticity to attract many viewers consistently and can motivate others to expand their social reach. An influencer may be anyone from a blogger to a celebrity to an online entrepreneur. They must simply capitalize on a niche to attain widespread credibility.[9]

How broad is their reach? Rivera says the Daily Dose is a motivational site that reaches 200 million people, one out of four people who use Instagram worldwide. Huda Kattan is the world's most influential beauty expert with 29 million followers. Cameron Dallas has 21 million who follow him to see his videos on a range of subjects. And Kayla Itsines has 10.5 million who look at her personal workout videos and inspiring messages.[10]

You and I probably aren't stars on YouTube, but all of us have the opportunity to pour ourselves into the lives of others with a specific goal of helping them have an ongoing impact. From person to person, we *pay it forward* and see lives changed. It can start small and become something incredibly important. Jesus started with twelve men, and in the next few generations, their impact swept through the Roman world. Pastors, business leaders, and people who have any position of influence can expand their reach by investing in the lives of a few. Scouts look for uniquely gifted athletes to recruit for sports teams, from baseball to cricket to gymnastics. They don't expect their own athletic talents to make a difference, and they aren't content to settle for the athletes already on the team. They're always looking for the next group of stars.

Parents and grandparents have wonderful opportunities to build character, hope, and courage into the lives of children. Kids are sponges who soak up the messages, verbal and non-verbal, communicated by those around them.

Two eminent psychologists give us perspective on the influence we have on our kids. Virginia Satir challenges us, "Every word, facial expression, gesture, or action on the part of a parent gives the child some message about self-worth. It is sad that so many parents don't realize what messages they are sending."[11]

And Brené Brown captures the heart of most of us:

I'm not a parenting expert. In fact, I'm not sure that I even believe in the idea of "parenting experts." I'm an engaged, imperfect parent and a passionate researcher. I'm an experienced mapmaker and a stumbling traveler. Like many of you, parenting is by far my boldest and most daring adventure.[12]

As we impart our values, hopes, vision, and skills to people, we need to remember that it took us plenty of time to make progress, at least at first. Whether you're mentoring a child, a team member, or someone in your small group, don't heap responsibility on them and overwhelm them. Invest in time to train, check up, and ease them into new things. You'll discover, if you haven't already, that some people thrive on challenges and some wilt under them. Discern the difference in the people you influence, and tailor your input to fit each person's motivational style and capacity to handle challenges. You'll save yourself time and money in the long run, and you'll raise the probability that your efforts will succeed in producing a new influencer.

> **AS WE IMPART OUR VALUES, HOPES, VISION, AND SKILLS TO PEOPLE, WE NEED TO REMEMBER THAT IT TOOK US PLENTY OF TIME TO MAKE PROGRESS, AT LEAST AT FIRST.**

CHALLENGE AND PACE

As we've seen, some people are tough and resilient, and others are impressionable and fragile, but everyone thrives on a greater vision of the future. As leaders, parents, and friends, if we push too hard, we may inspire some of these people for a while, but we risk crushing their spirits. But for those who are go-getters, if we're too slow, too cautious, or too timid, they'll find someone else who will throw the match of vision into their gasoline of passion. As we relate to different people, one size definitely doesn't fit all. I've known very gifted and committed people who gave everything they had to fulfill their responsibilities, and when they felt pressured to do more, they soon reached their breaking point and crumbled under the stress. They were doing as much as they could as soon as they could, but going farther and faster was too much for them. But I've also known people who had tremendous, latent talents that weren't brought out until their boss or parent said something like, "You're not living up to your potential. You're so much better than this.

Come on, get going. Do something great!" It's crucial to know the difference between these two types of people.

Many organizational leaders rose to their positions by reaching, pushing, and striving for bigger and better. Now, they come into every meeting with the conviction that every person can do more—sometimes a lot more. There's certainly nothing wrong with pointing people to greater heights, but some of these leaders don't see the range of motivations in the room. All they see is a room full of nails, so the only tool they use is their hammer.

The Great Commission was the most audacious vision in history, and we see Christians in the early church giving everything they've got to the cause. Luke's account illustrates the enormous challenge, the patient pace, and the crucial decisions made by the leaders of the early church. For instance, thousands were saved at Pentecost and in the months that followed, but the disciples understood that all of these new believers needed nurturing and teaching, so they gathered them into small groups. (See Acts 2.)

Launching the church pushed the disciples to the limit. At one point, they realized they were overlooking some Greek women who were new believers. (See Acts 6:1.) Instead of blaming the Greeks for complaining, they adjusted their leadership structure to care for them. Not long after that, Stephen spoke out boldly and he paid the ultimate price of being stoned to death. (See Acts 7.)

Saul was an accomplice in the execution and worked to destroy the church, but Jesus met him on the road to Damascus and changed the trajectory of his life. (See Acts 9.) He immediately proved he was completely devoted to Christ by preaching about salvation through Jesus in the synagogue in Damascus until he too came under threat of capture and death. When the disciples in Jerusalem didn't trust this new convert's story, Barnabas stood up for him. The leaders realized his faith was genuine, but he posed a threat wherever he went, so they sent him home to Tarsus. Luke tells us, *"Then the church throughout Judea, Galilee and Samaria enjoyed a time of peace and was strengthened. Living in the fear of the Lord and encouraged by the Holy Spirit, it increased in numbers"* (Acts 9:31).

As we step into the lives of the people we lead or the children we parent, we need to understand who needs challenge and who thrives on affirmation. To some degree, everyone needs both, but they feel understood, affirmed, and encouraged to do their best when we understand their specific desire.

> **AS WE STEP INTO THE LIVES OF THE PEOPLE WE LEAD OR THE CHILDREN WE PARENT, WE NEED TO UNDERSTAND WHO NEEDS CHALLENGE AND WHO THRIVES ON AFFIRMATION.**

Certainly, use challenge to raise people's sights, but provide a realistic pace for change and growth, especially for those who are more sensitive. It has been said that if a leader is ten steps ahead of people, he becomes a martyr because so many people criticize him, but if he's two steps ahead, he's a visionary shepherd—the very best kind of leader.

UNITY AND DISAGREEMENT

Some people completely misunderstand the concept of unity. They assume that voicing concerns or disagreement necessarily destroys unity, but that's not the case. Healthy disagreement sharpens our minds, clarifies our purpose, and shapes our direction. Without it, we become stagnant; with it, each person on the team or in the family can excel.

A friend of mine—I'll call him Dan—was on the board of a nonprofit. For weeks, the board members debated how to handle the failure of their CEO to lead the organization. The dozen people, most of whom were recruited because they were able and willing to donate generously to the nonprofit, were split in their perception of the CEO, and their discussions had become more heated over time. Finally, the board chairman called for a meeting to resolve the issue one way or another.

As the meeting started, Dan whispered to another board member, "We'll see how people handle disagreements tonight. I hope people feel free to say what they need to say." After the meeting had been going for only about fifteen minutes and a couple of people had cautiously shared their convictions, one of the board members said in a tone of exasperation, "This isn't right! We shouldn't have this kind of disagreement. We should just stop the meeting, cool off, and come back in a better frame of mind."

The board chairman looked confused. He hesitated for a minute and then said, "Well, okay. We'll come back next week and see if we can make progress toward a decision."

The man sitting next to Dan looked relieved. He told Dan, "Wow, that sure lowered the level of tension in the room, didn't it?"

Dan replied, "Is that the goal of the meeting? Sometimes, we have to wade into the tension instead of doing whatever it takes to eliminate it." He paused for a second and then explained, "All that did was postpone the hard conversation we need to have. That guy feels powerful, the chairman feels confused, and the rest of us missed an opportunity to be honest with each other."

UNITY BINDS PEOPLE DESPITE THEIR DIFFERENCES, WHILE UNIFORMITY SEEKS TO ELIMINATE ALL DIFFERENCES.

There's a great difference between unity and uniformity. The former binds people despite their differences; the latter seeks to eliminate all differences, relying on force to bring change or achieve objectives. Disagreement is certainly a threat to uniformity, but that shouldn't be our goal. Differing opinions, even strongly expressed, don't destroy unity…unless people assume they do.

Healthy disagreement focuses on ideas, not the person. In other words, don't engage in *ad hominem* attacks; that means avoiding the use of *you statements* in the discussion. Even then, it's important to avoid blasting the idea. Instead, focus on the strengths of the idea and try to find ways to make it better. Rather than saying, "Yes, but…," say, "Yes, and…" Don't assume that a person who disagrees with you is somehow not only wrong, but also foolish and bad.

I've been in meetings when disagreements became too personal and too heated. Instead of letting it go on and trying to navigate the choppy waters, I stopped and said, "We'll come back to the issue in a few minutes, but before then, let's talk about what's happening in the room right now." I then spend time training the people about how to have healthy disagreements that build the team instead of destroying it. When we come back to the issue that sparked the intense debate, if people are still violating the norms I've just given them, I tell them, "Let's stop right here. We can think about this for a week. Maybe next time we can have a very honest conversation without the additional baggage of blame and suspicion. But first, we're going to talk about the values of humility, listening, and respect. If we don't get that right, we can't have honest conversations. All we'll do is manipulate each other, and I'm not willing for us to do that any longer."

Brian King, a business analyst and consultant, observes:

Ask any great business leader about the process which led to some of their best and most important decisions made, and you will likely hear about the arguments, disagreements and contested discussions among a leadership team, all of which led to final decisions and course of action. I remember a number of these instances in my company as well, and the times I had to remind myself to tolerate, consider, and accept the challenges and questions about my opinion and decisions.[13]

GREAT LEADERS INVITE PEOPLE TO CHALLENGE THEIR IDEAS, BUT THEY DON'T CAVE IN TO ADOPT THE CONVICTIONS OF EVERY PERSON ON THE TEAM.

In companies, churches, nonprofits, and families, uniformity isn't a worthy goal. Great leaders invite people to challenge their ideas, but they don't cave in to adopt the convictions of every person on the team. These leaders are secure enough to welcome disagreement, and they're skilled enough to make it produce an outcome that moves the organization or family forward and makes each person involved feel valued. A measure of disagreement is an inescapable tension in leading people.

THE TEAM AND INDIVIDUALS

Leaders live in the tension between what's best for the team and what's best for an individual on the team. Sometimes, an assignment is given to everyone, but often, it is delegated to one person who marshals resources to accomplish the goal.

For years, I've taught leaders that their systems are at least as important as the people on their teams. The system is how the team functions: how it's organized, how it makes decisions, how it carries out those decisions, how it communicates, and how it gets accurate feedback. The system is the vehicle the team members drive toward their objectives.

The following chart shows the tension points between systems and team members:

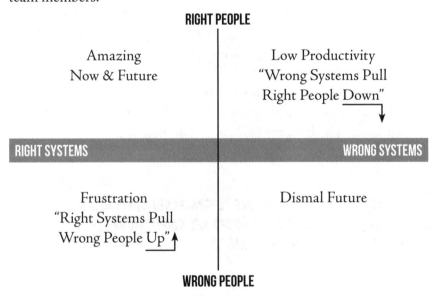

+ Right systems and right people work in harmony and are very productive.

+ Right systems pull wrong people up.

+ Wrong systems pull right people down.

+ Wrong systems and wrong people result in a train wreck.

Most of us in business, the church, or nonprofits need to analyze our systems far more rigorously. We live with them year after year because they're part of the history of our organizations—"the way we've always done things"—but they may not be as effective as they could be. We're wise to take nothing for granted, to read, to study, to hire a consultant, and to do whatever it takes to refine or reconstruct our systems of operations so they're more effective.

And we need to take a long, hard look at the names on the organizational chart. As organizations grow, some people grow in their capacity and capabilities. But many can't keep up with the added responsibilities. We don't necessarily need to fire people, but we may need to move them to a role where their talents and capacity fit in the organization. These are hard decisions, but it's a tension every growing organization faces.

The solution isn't to focus on only one or the other, systems or staff, but to have the courage to ask the hard questions about both.

FAMILIAR AND DISTANT

As an organization grows, the leader reaches the limits of familiarity in relationships. A pastor or business leader may recognize the faces and recall the names of a hundred or even two hundred people, but beyond that point, faces and names become a blur. That's not a flaw; it's just a reality. Some leaders feel so uncomfortable with this fact that they never want to grow beyond the circle of people they know and call friends or colleagues. Beyond that point, leaders need to assess virtually everything they do to be sure someone (besides them) is meeting the needs of those outside their circle. Each element of the system, the protocols, the structure and people in meetings, standard operating procedures, reporting, and the leadership team needs scrutiny and adjustments.

With growth comes inevitable pushback. In companies, suppliers and customers who have enjoyed personal attention from the owner wonder why they're now contacted by someone else. As a church grows, people who felt close to the pastor may find they aren't *in the loop* any longer. They complain, "He used to come to our Fourth of July barbeque, but he doesn't come now," "He used to do all the weddings, but now he does only a few," or "I used to have his phone number and could call him any time, but he changed his number and didn't give it to me." They want the same level of familiarity they enjoyed in the past, and they're disappointed that it's gone. A few customers and parishioners leave, which is part of the price of growth.

> **IT'S VERY DIFFICULT FOR SOME ENTREPRENEURS AND PASTORS TO SEE THEIR ORGANIZATIONS GROW BEYOND THE POINT WHERE THEY'RE INVOLVED IN EVERY DECISION AND THEY HAVE A HAND IN MEETING EVERY NEED.**

It's very difficult for some entrepreneurs and pastors to see their organizations grow beyond the point where they're involved in every decision and they have a hand in meeting every need. Their challenge is to change from the primary role of shepherding to the very different role of an executive. As the systems change, they have to change, too. There isn't a right or wrong here: it's perfectly acceptable for leaders to choose to keep their organizations at a size they can manage without significant change. Today, the leaders who are famous and asked to speak at events are pastors of megachurches and entrepreneurs who have built large businesses—and everyone is overtly or covertly compared to them. For this reason, many leaders feel enormous pressure to abandon their God-given gifts of shepherding to compete with those remarkable leaders who are, in actuality, outliers in their fields.

Leaders—and especially pastors, but also parents—live in the tension between familiarity and distance: they can't get too close, or they lose their authority, but they can't get too far away or they'll lose their heart connection with people.

THREE OPTIONS

I can't count the number of times a leader has told me a story about a relationship problem, on the job or at home, and finished by asking, "Sam, help me out. What can I do about this?"

It's a great question, one that all of us instinctively ask when we wade into difficult moments in relationships. I believe we have three options:

1. EMBRACE THE TENSION

As we've seen so far in this book, tension isn't the enemy...at least, we don't need to see it that way. Some of us create chaos to control people, and many others avoid conflict at all cost because it makes us feel so uncomfortable. One option (one that many people don't consider) is to live with it, to embrace it as an inevitable reality. If we expect life to be neat and each element to always be in the right boxes, we'll be deeply distressed when we get married and have children! Some level of tension is just part of life, and we're wise to embrace it.

2. RESOLVE THE TENSION

When conflict, stress, or chaos is *over the red line*, it's time to wade in and at least bring the level down to an acceptable level. In these instances, it's up to us to do all we can to engage the person, share our concerns, listen well, listen even more, and look for ways to move forward. But let me be clear: resolving tension isn't a one-person show. *Both* people—or *all* involved if there are more than two—need to be willing to engage, communicate, listen, and advance. If the other person refuses, that's on him, not you. Of course, not all tension is interpersonal. We may experience difficulties in health, finances, mental clarity, and many other possible sources of tension. Some of these can't be resolved, but we may be able to limit the damage with creative and compassionate solutions.

3. USE THE TENSION

The best lessons are learned in the crucible of difficulty. These moments cause our adrenaline to flow, our minds to become sharper, and our determination to grow. We can use these stress-filled times as *learning opportunities* for us and for the people who are watching us, but we'll miss these moments if we're immobilized by either anger or fear. Using the tension requires us to step back, breathe deeply, and do some careful analysis. Only then will we realize the golden opportunities hidden within the difficulties.

Relationships are the glue that hold families and organizations together, and they're the foundation of stability so people can be launched into a greater future. We experience inevitable tensions, even in our strongest relationships. We're wise to recognize them and use them to make the connections even stronger.

THINK ABOUT IT:

1. Have you ever been on a team or in a family when one person dominated everyone's attention by being negative and critical? How did this person affect others, especially you?

2. Who are you pouring your life into to help them become influencers? What is your hope for these people?

3. Who is a leader or parent you know who tailors communication to people who need more challenge and those who need a less pressured pace? How are you doing with this tension in your relationships?

4. What are some ways people respond when they feel personally attacked in disagreements? What is one principle from this section that you can apply in disagreements with people in your family or on your team?

5. Whether you're a leader in a church or business, or you're a parent, how would you describe the effect of your systems (communication, decision-making process, reporting, etc.) on the people you lead? What, if anything, needs to change?

6. It's certainly possible for any of us to become too familiar or too distant with the people around us. How can we know if we're too far one way or the other?

APPLY IT:

* As you read this chapter, what tensions described here reminded you of your experiences?

* How did you respond at the time?

* How do you want to respond next time?

* Who do you know who is experiencing a similar tension today?

* How can you help this person embrace the tension, resolve the tension, or use the tension to stimulate an innovative solution?

3

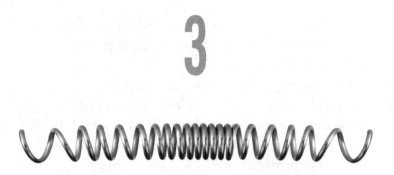

YOU CAN'T ESCAPE IT

Creativity arises out of the tension between
spontaneity and limitations.
—Rollo May

Years ago, when I was leading an organization, my executive team consisted of five vice presidents. I use the term *team* cautiously because our meetings had multiple dramas going on at the same time. Two of the people on our team often walked in with obvious tension between them. They had a long history of resentment toward each other that was seldom concealed. Another person had been suffering from serious illness for over a year. He was giving it everything he had, but he was so understandably preoccupied with his illness that we never knew if his mind was completely with us. The other two were *alpha* leaders who always had the right answer, could always accomplish the goal, and never made a mistake (at least in their view). I valued their talents and tenacity, and they got a lot done, but their insistence on being the top dog often rubbed people the wrong way…including me.

Sounds like a lot of fun, doesn't it?

For every item on our agenda each week, I had to anticipate how each person would respond—not only to the idea but even more to each other. There were power plays within power plays. In addition, each one brought the pressure of their own team's expectations. They often promised them certain outcomes to our discussions, so they were anything but objective as we discussed the intricacies of each topic.

They were devoted to the status quo and often fiercely resisted innovation. I'm known now—and was known then—as an entrepreneur. My ideas often shook them up, even when I carefully explained the concepts, the benefits, and the process of implementation.

But there was one other factor that complicated our staff meetings and caused the level of tension to soar: alliances. On the most important topics, these five men formed partnerships to promote their ideas and torpedo those who had a different agenda—and the alliances shifted depending on the topic. Some of them seemed to be very traditional in their views of leadership, strictly following the accepted industry protocols to make decisions and implement them, but others were impatient with this laborious process. The alliances could be formed around a principle, a concept, a program, or a person who showed promise or was proving to be a problem. I soon realized that for these five vice presidents, every meeting was actually three meetings: the meeting before the meeting when they formed their alliances, the meeting itself where the allied people supported and defended each other, and the meeting after the meeting with their allies to plot their next steps. By far, the most important of these three was the meeting before the meeting, when they were crafting their battle plan. It didn't take me very long to form a mental spreadsheet to keep track of how I expected each person to respond to each topic in each staff meeting. It seemed necessary, but it was exhausting.

I'm not the only one who learned to anticipate each person's response to every point. Our meetings became a game of chess played on a board with six individuals, but almost always with pairs playing together against all the rest.

> **IN ANY ORGANIZATION, PAY ATTENTION TO THE "MEETING BEFORE THE MEETING," WHEN ALLIANCES ARE FORMED AND BATTLE PLANS ARE CRAFTED.**

I learned that it was often counterproductive to ask for votes on issues. Instead, I looked for *the sense of the room.* I spent a lot of time giving directions to each person about how I expected them to communicate the decisions. I knew they could say the right words, but in a tone that communicated that they were against it.

As the leader, I felt plenty of pressure to move the organization forward. I had plans and dreams, and these five men were my team. For a long time—far too long—I tried to keep everyone on the team happy and productive without addressing *the elephant in the room.* I knew that if I said, "Hey, let's talk about what's going on here," there would be fierce reactions, defensiveness, and self-justification. In other words, things would get even worse.

As I look back on that period, I recall that for a while, I wondered if the tension was a result of my poor leadership. Maybe I didn't know how to lead meetings like this, or maybe this situation was categorically different from any other realm. Maybe our policies were out of date and the interpersonal stress was a result of our administrative policies lagging behind. But at a crucial point, I realized I was spending a lot of time trying to manage the competing agendas of these five vice presidents, and my preoccupation with their probable reactions consumed my thoughts far beyond the actual meetings.

Finally, I had the insight and courage to address the problem. In a particular staff meeting—one that was no different from the rest except that I was determined to speak the truth to them—I recognized one man's passionate plea for his ideas, another's defensiveness, and the obvious alliances that had already been formed before this conversation, and I said, "Let me stop us right here. What's going on in this meeting?"

There was a very awkward silence.

A BETTER ANGLE

Many people see tension as a threat. They feel their adrenaline level rise, their emotions become more intense, and their thinking often becomes clouded at the very moment they need greater clarity. It doesn't have to be this way. We need to see tension from a different angle so it works for us instead of against us.

If we believe that the optimum life should be completely devoid of tension, we'll be confused, disappointed, and resentful of those people and events that disrupt our perfect peace. As leaders and parents, our goal isn't to relieve all tension, but instead to use it constructively.

We can define tension in a number of ways. Some define it negatively:

+ Tension is the inevitable result when people feel unsafe, disempowered, blamed, or ignored.[14]

+ When things feel so tight they might snap.[15]

+ But it can also be seen as neutral or positive:

+ Tension is the balance between equally valid points of view, and conflict is what comes from losing that balance.[16]

+ "Creative tension" is the feeling or process we all have to go through to get from A to B and achieve our creative goals.[17]

Over time, I became less confused when I encountered tension and I developed the ability to use it in positive, healthy, productive ways instead of letting it erode my confidence, sap my energy, and reduce the effectiveness of a team. Now, when I sense tension, I become more reflective, and I listen more than I defend my positions. I listen for what is said, as well as what isn't being said. I watch body language to see if it validates or conflicts with the person's words. My goalposts have moved from controlling and reducing the tension to understanding and using it. From this perspective, tension is no longer the enemy; it's a path to greater insight, stronger relationships, and better outcomes.

WHEN YOU UNDERSTAND AND USE TENSION, IT'S A PATH TO GREATER INSIGHT, STRONGER RELATIONSHIPS, AND BETTER OUTCOMES.

At the organization with the five vice presidents, my new view of tension gave our team a different set of rules. In one way, it became safer to voice disagreements because it was perfectly acceptable to have differing points of view, but I challenged them when I saw them form alliances, demand their own way, and exhibit self-protective behaviors. We put the chessboard away and became more honest about our previously unspoken but very real agendas.

I realized that tension is normal, neutral, and natural. I don't have to be afraid of it, I don't need to assume I'm defective when I encounter it, and I don't have to make it my primary goal to relieve it. If my goal is to eliminate tension, I'll focus on appeasing people instead of leading them. With these insights, I have a wide range of options. Most often, I can *use* the tension to stimulate creativity, but I may also choose to *confront* the tension if it persists between people, or I may *ignore* the tension if I sense that someone is simply having a bad day.

Years ago, my wife Brenda and I went to the top of the Space Needle in Seattle, Washington, to celebrate our first wedding anniversary and have a nice dinner in the revolving restaurant. We enjoyed watching the views of the city, Mount Rainier, and Puget Sound. It was a windy day… at least it was windy at the altitude of six hundred feet. The restaurant swayed noticeably in the wind, and we were more than a little nervous. When a waiter walked by, I asked, "Excuse me. We feel the wind blowing the Space Needle. Is it…is it normal?" My real question was, "Are you as scared as we are?"

He smiled. "Yes, it's completely normal," he assured us. "The engineers built it to sway so it wouldn't break and collapse."

That was comforting…sort of. But he was right. Structural engineers build tension points into bridges and other buildings to account for wind, temperature variations, and earth movements, especially earthquakes.

For us, too, recognizing and using our tension points can actually bring stability and strength. And they can keep us from collapsing!

NO EXCEPTIONS

Who needs a more positive view of tension? *All of us.* When do we need it? All the time, in every relationship. Couples can use the inevitable tension of competing goals to draw them closer instead of driving a wedge between them. Parents can use the disagreements with their kids to promote understanding instead of resentment and isolation. Team members can learn to harness the tension among them to produce better ideas and heightened harmony. Leaders can create healthy tension that brings out the best in every person instead of letting suspicion and distrust create a toxic environment.

WHEN A FAMILY, AN EXECUTIVE TEAM, A DEPARTMENT, OR A BIBLE STUDY GROUP USES TENSION TO STIMULATE RICH CONVERSATIONS AND GROWTH, AMAZING THINGS CAN HAPPEN.

When a family, an executive team, a department, or a Bible study group uses tension to stimulate rich conversations and growth, amazing things can happen. But it only takes one person in these settings to throw a wrench into the machinery. The danger is that someone will react by trying to reduce the tension because it feels too unsettling; hide emotionally or physically to avoid the unpleasant feelings; or dominate others to eliminate the sense of being out of control. But of course, if people in the family, team, or group have developed the skill of creatively using tension, they won't take the bait of joining an alliance. They'll address the situation boldly and lovingly so the confused or disruptive person has a chance to learn and grow.

We often make one of two mistakes in dealing with people who respond to tension by appeasing, hiding, or dominating: we either say too little or say too much. We say too little when we talk about anything and everything but the unhealthy tension in the room. We may claim that we want to be *harmless as doves* and *not rock the boat*, but our lack of forthrightness leaves the rest of the people concerned that we don't see what they see, or if they know we see it, we're too cowardly to do anything about it. But some of us are on the other end of the continuum: we say too much. I've found that if someone is reacting out of character in a meeting, I usually don't have to step in to confront him. He probably needs more comfort than correction. When I tailor my words and actions to communicate understanding and support, most of the time, the person apologizes and becomes a productive team member again.

IMPORTANT RELATIONSHIPS

Let's briefly examine how we experience tension in our most important relationships:

COUPLES

Couples have normal tensions around some very common issues, including how they handle money, relate to in-laws, and raise their children. In many cases, they have different (and even opposite) points of view. These can become battlegrounds, or they can become gyms where the relationship becomes stronger.

FAMILIES

Families experience tension in innumerable ways: preferences for food, sports, time, attention, communication style and frequency, games, vacations, and school performance. Even seemingly simple decisions about where to stay on a vacation can arouse competing desires related to comfort, amenities, and cost. The stages of family life create different tensions. Psychologists have identified several stages in the life cycle of families, but for our purposes, we'll focus on three:

- The *beginning* of a family is the courtship and wedding, including the years before the first child is born. In this stage, the couple has to learn to navigate the differences in how they spend their time and their money, and they need to work out their differing preferences in a host of choices.

- The *expanding* stage consists of the years between the time when children are born and when they leave the nest. These years are full of hopes and dreams, time pressures, and adjustments in expectations. Each new birth doesn't add only a single set of tensions; it multiplies the tensions throughout the matrix of the family.

- The *contracting* stage is one of celebration and heartache. The parents may have to redefine themselves and their relationship after the children are gone, adult children may require more assistance than was expected, financial mistakes earlier in the marriage may now create worries as they near retirement, health problems may multiply, and caring for aging parents may add to the tensions the couple experiences. And yet the aging couple can take immeasurable satisfaction when they see their children and grandchildren thrive.

Many families live with the hard realities of divorce. The word is freighted with meaning because it implies radical disruption of the most treasured relationship. The damage goes far beyond the nuclear family and has a ripple effect on friends, who often feel they need to take sides, and on parents or siblings of the couple, who may blame one and exonerate the other (and not always who we might expect). The kids, no matter their ages, feel the brunt of the chaos and need ways to process their powerful feelings.

An important study on tension points in family and career assigned scores to the causes of tension based on the impact they had on the study's participants. The baseline was the death of a spouse at 100 points. The other *usual suspects* were divorce at 73 points, being imprisoned at 63, and being fired at work at 47. But other life events that are considered to be very positive also created significant levels of tension: marriage at 50 points, retirement at 45, birth of a child at 39, and outstanding personal achievement at 28. The study's authors conclude: "Remarkably, there is little disagreement about these values among raters differing in age, sex, marital status, education, social class, race, and creed. In addition, there was substantial agreement among people from different cultures. Swedes, Danes, Japanese, and North Americans appeared to regard the impact of life changes in similar ways."[18]

> **THE SOURCES OF TENSION HIT ALL OF US IN VIRTUALLY THE SAME WAYS WITH THE SAME FORCE AND EVEN THE MOST POSITIVE EVENTS CREATE SUBSTANTIAL TENSION.**

In other words, the sources of tension hit all of us in virtually the same ways with the same force and even the most positive events in our lives create substantial tension.

Research reported by the American Institute of Stress is alarming. For instance, 77 percent of people "regularly experience physical symptoms caused by stress," 73 percent "regularly experience psychological symptoms" such as depression and anxiety, 76 percent "cited money and work as the leading cause of their stress," and 48 percent "reported lying awake at night due to stress."[19] (The institute offers a free stress assessment at: www.stress.org/self-assessment.)

Although we need to accept the fact that tension is a fact of life, passivity isn't the remedy. Especially in our most important relationships, we need to assertively and wisely take steps to resolve the tension: talking, listening, listening even more, forgiving, and finding a way forward. However, when the current tension is resolved, we face the next set when we intuitively ask, "What's next in the relationship?"

WORK OR CHURCH

At work or in church, as a staff member or a volunteer, we come with different backgrounds and goals, and we often have hidden agendas—hidden even from ourselves. If we're not careful, we can develop the habit of reacting by pleasing, hiding, or dominating, by building alliances or trying to manipulate others to get our way. A better perspective on tension lowers our blood pressure and makes us less reactive and more optimistic, more affirming of people who disagree with us, and more understanding of their points of view. Instead of reacting in defiance, self-protection, and self-promotion, we slow down, ask good questions, and become better listeners. We're more approachable and we delight when others are successful. We become *brand carriers* for the organization as we reframe challenges as opportunities, look for advantages in every situation, and take action instead of wasting time blaming others.

THINK ABOUT IT:

1. What are some situations and relationships when you experienced a significant level of tension? How did you respond to each one?

2. How would you define tension?

3. What harm does it do to expect to live a tension-free life? Do you know anyone who has this expectation? What are the results?

4. What are some tensions you've experienced from positive events? Did you expect the intensity of the stress that came from the unresolved tension? How did you handle it?

5. What difference would it make for you to see *creative tension* as an asset instead of a threat?

6. What is your hope in reading this book?

APPLY IT:

+   As you read this chapter, what tensions described here reminded you of your experiences?

+   How did you respond at the time?

+   How do you want to respond next time?

+   Who do you know who is experiencing a similar tension today?

+   How can you help this person embrace the tension, resolve the tension, or use the tension to stimulate an innovative solution?

4

IT'S YOUR CHOICE

You must not only learn to live with tension,
you must seek it out. You must learn to thrive on stress.
—J. Paul Getty

I grew up in Lucknow, a city in the northern part of India. My parents had high hopes for me. My father was a respected pastor and he wanted to provide me with the finest education as a launching pad for the rest of my life. He spent more than a quarter of his income to send me to St. Francis High School, a prestigious Catholic parochial school.

I failed the tenth grade. In fact, I failed every class that year. Whenever a friend asked me to skip school and have some fun, I was ready to go. Every morning, I got dressed and left the house with my books, but more often than not, I didn't make it through the front door of the school. I assured my parents that I was doing well in school. At the end of every term, I was given a report card to show my parents. Miraculously, the F's turned into A's before they saw the report card. They thought I was doing exceptionally well, and they were pleased.

Finally, the bottom dropped out. My final report card had the usual string of F's in every subject, so I would have to repeat the grade. I couldn't lie my way out of that one, so I took the report card home and handed it to them. They expected to see the glowing evidence of my academic excellence, but when they looked at the report card, their smiles turned to shock. It took a while for it all to sink in, but they soon realized the bitter truth—and they were humiliated. India is a shame and honor culture, so the actions of each family member reflect on everyone else. And bad news travels fast: soon, all of our neighbors knew that I had failed and would have to repeat the tenth grade. I had brought tremendous shame to my family, especially to my father. In India, one person's success or failure colors the reputation of the entire family—and it's a dishonor that often remains for generations. At the end of that year, people looked at my father and his church with a different and darker perception. In addition to the shame, my father had sacrificed to pay for me to go to the school, and all of this money had been wasted.

AFTER A YEAR OF SKIPPING SCHOOL AND BRINGING DISHONOR TO MY FAMILY, THE TENSION I HAD CREATED FOR MYSELF SEEMED CRUSHING AND UNALTERABLE.

My parents didn't want me to stay at St. Francis and repeat the tenth grade. Everyone in the school would know, and they would talk; everyone in our community knew, and they were already talking. A few months later, I enrolled in a different high school, but that year, my assurances that I was doing well in my classes were met with understandable skepticism and a barrage of piercing questions about my study habits, attendance, and grades.

Do I know anything about tension? Yes, I have some experience with it. At that point in my life, things looked very bleak. I had brought dishonor on my family, which was the worst thing a young man could do. If someone had come up to me at that time and said, "Sam, one day you'll be the president of a college in the United States," I would have wondered about his sanity, or I would have asked, "What are you smoking?" For me, a destiny of success was simply inconceivable. The tension I had created for myself seemed crushing and unalterable.

SOURCES AND COMPLEXITIES

At this point, some of you who are reading this book are thinking, *Man, he's reading my mind! I need these perspectives about the tension in my life.* But others are having a different reaction. You're thinking, *Sam, you don't get it. You've talked about "creative tension," but the tension in my life is killing me! It doesn't feel all that creative!*

> **IF OUR HOPE IS TO SEE GOD USE THE TENSION TO PRODUCE SOMETHING GOOD, SOMETHING NOBLE, AND SOMETHING OF LASTING VALUE, WE CAN HAVE ASSURANCE THAT HE WILL COME THROUGH.**

We've already identified a wide range of the sources of tension: relationships at home, pressures at work, health problems, financial struggles, the turmoil of raising teenagers, and even the added stress of very positive events like births, graduations, and marriages. The problem is that the tensions can multiply and eventually feel overwhelming. The pressure we encounter may come not from the normal issues of being flawed people who live in a fallen world, but by our own unwise choices, the foolish choices of others close to us, and, especially, by unrealistic expectations that *life shouldn't be this hard* or *God will protect me from trouble*—and when He doesn't, we can be shattered by the disappointment.

If our highest hope is to be completely free of tension, our misplaced expectation will multiply our difficulties and make us deeply discouraged. But if our hope is to see God use the tension to produce something good, something noble, and something of lasting value, we can have assurance that He will come through…in His way…and in His timing.

OUR CHOICES DETERMINE THE OUTCOME

Every moment of every day, we can choose how we respond to tension. Our choices determine whether it destroys us or strengthens us.

TENSION DESTROYS WHEN...

YOU GET ANGRY AND FRUSTRATED THAT YOU CAN'T FIGURE IT ALL OUT.

You assume you can think your way out of tension, and you use your intelligence and wit to try to stay on top of things. There's certainly nothing wrong with thinking and reasoning, but some people believe they can think long enough and hard enough to relieve all the tension they feel.

YOU PRESSURE PEOPLE TO ACT LIKE THERE'S NO TENSION.

A team leader tells his staff to put on a smile when they walk out of the room, even though they've just had a knock-down, drag-out disagreement. A couple walks into a party holding hands and smiling, but they've hardly spoken to each other in the past week.

YOU HAVE A "SUPERMAN COMPLEX" AND ASSUME YOU CAN FIX
EVERY PERSON AND EVERY SITUATION.

Many people are *compulsive fixers* who get their self-worth from their attempts to right every wrong and make people do the right thing. We often applaud these people because they are so *helpful*, but they can rob recipients of their dignity and prevent them from learning to be responsible.

YOU USE BULLYING TACTICS TO GET YOUR WAY.

Some people try to manage tension by *getting big*—talking loudly, glaring menacingly, and demanding compliance from everyone they know. The people who are the targets of their demands often *get little*, cowering and giving in to avoid more attacks.

YOU ESCAPE TO AVOID THE TENSION.

To avoid thinking and feeling, people may watch hours and hours of television, read, or do almost anything to occupy their minds.

YOU AVOID HAVING ANY OPINIONS BECAUSE YOU'RE AFRAID
OF BEING BLASTED AS WRONG.

Some people feel overwhelmed by the oppressive tension in their lives, and they try to cope by not having an opinion about anything. Stating their opinion would open them up to criticism, and they can't stand that.

YOU SULK TO GET ATTENTION AND BE PITIED.

Some people play the victim card, hoping others will cater to them and not ask them to do anything hard, like producing what they're responsible for.

YOU SELF-MEDICATE TO NUMB THE PAIN.

People may use alcohol, drugs, gambling, food, or almost any substance or behavior to mask the tension they don't want to face.

PEOPLE ARE AFRAID TO SPEAK THE TRUTH TO YOU BECAUSE YOU'RE EITHER TOO FRAGILE OR A BULLY.

Tension that isn't addressed with wisdom and truth can quickly shatter trust through a violent outburst or slowly erode trust through isolation and criticism. The results of a lack of trust are the extremes of being fragile or being a bully. Either way, the message to others is, "Don't talk to me about anything important. I'll either crumble under it, or I'll use it against you."

YOU FEEL TRAPPED BECAUSE YOU DON'T SEE ANY OTHER CHOICES.

Perhaps the most common way tension destroys is when people don't believe they have any options in how to deal with it. They feel like prisoners in their homes and at work.

TENSION STRENGTHENS WHEN...

YOU SEE IT AS AN OPPORTUNITY INSTEAD OF A THREAT.

Instead of instantly catastrophizing—thinking, *The world is coming to an end!*—it's possible to slow down and ask, "What are some positive outcomes that can happen from this?" You won't find them if you don't look for them.

YOU BECOME MORE AWARE OF OTHERS' FEELINGS AND YOUR SURROUNDINGS.

When tension isn't a threat, we don't suffer from tunnel vision. Our range of vision expands; we become more observant, noticing words, tone, and gestures. We see how people are reacting to each other. Our goal is no longer to get the tension over as quickly as possible, but to use it for good in every person's life.

YOU LEARN TO MAKE ADJUSTMENTS IN THE MOMENT.

With time and practice, we're more fully present in each situation and conversation, and we respond in the moment instead of having to think about it for hours or days after the crucial encounter has passed.

YOU BECOME WISER, MORE PATIENT, AND KINDER.

When we react to the perceived threat of a tense moment with fight, flight, or freezing, our focus is on protecting ourselves or dominating the other people. As we gain a better perspective, we learn to notice the truth beneath the surface, we're patient instead of insistent because we know what it's like to be reactionary, and we have compassion for those who are under the weight of multiplied tension.

YOU GIVE OTHERS THE BENEFIT OF THE DOUBT.

As our confidence grows, we no longer insist on being right all the time. We value opposing opinions, and we aren't surprised when people verbalize them a little too passionately or a little too hesitantly.

YOU LISTEN CAREFULLY TO PEOPLE WHO DISAGREE WITH YOU OR OPPOSE YOU.

When we feel stressed, we just want relief—and we want it now! In these circumstances, we want people to hear us, and we're not eager to hear them. But as we learn how to use tension for good, we listen intently to others to understand their concepts, their feelings, and their goals.

YOUR BRAIN CHEMISTRY REINFORCES A HEALTHY PATTERN OF RESPONSES.

Our brains are wired with feedback loops. This means that unhealthy patterns replicate themselves, but brain chemicals also reinforce positive behaviors. A study of military Special Forces showed that for many of the men and women, in tense situations such as combat, brain chemicals actually cause their minds to slow down so they can think more clearly and act with more precision. An author summarizes the findings: "In other words, when the going gets tough, you can mimic the brain activity of the bravest performers by adopting their mindset: look on the bright side and take decisive action."[20] Probably few of us are in the category of Navy SEALs, but the point is that our brains are wired to reinforce our choices.

YOU BECOME HUMBLE AND LESS JEALOUS.

Humility, as the saying goes, isn't thinking less of yourself, it's thinking of yourself less. When we feel threatened by tension, we become remarkably self-absorbed, but as we become wiser and stronger in our response to pressure-packed situations and difficult people, we feel more secure and less passionate about defending ourselves. We also no longer feel the need to compete to put ourselves up by putting others down.

YOU BECOME A GREAT EXAMPLE TO THE PEOPLE AROUND YOU.

One of the most powerful motivations for many of us is the realization that our responses to tension affect the people around us, especially our children, but also our spouses, colleagues, and friends.

FOR YEARS, MOST OF US HAVE LIVED AS IF WE HAD NO CHOICE IN HOW WE REACTED TO DIFFICULT SITUATIONS AND PEOPLE, BUT WE REALLY HAVE MANY OPTIONS.

OUR OPTIONS ABOUND

For years, most of us have lived as if we had no choice in how we reacted to difficult situations and people, but we really have many options. As we relax and our minds are clear, we *read the room* and notice what's going on better than ever before.

I remember one of the first times I was in a meeting when someone expressed emotions that were out of proportion to the topic we were discussing. I thought, *I wonder what that's all about?* I decided to wade in. I interrupted the person's diatribe and asked, "Would you tell me what's going on with you right now? Your emotions seem to be pretty strong. Am I missing something?"

He was surprised that I was responding by asking questions instead of opposing him. He turned to me and growled, "I'll tell you. Do you remember what happened the last time we tried this approach? I was left holding the bag because some other people didn't do their jobs."

He may have hoped that everyone, including me, would be cowed by his accusation, but I invited him, "Tell me more about what happened."

He launched into a detailed history of what had happened and who had failed. I could tell others in the room felt unfairly accused. Instead of letting the meeting dissolve into a finger-pointing match, I told him, "Thank you for giving us your perspective. I appreciate it." I turned to the group and asked, "So, what can we do next time that will be more productive?" In this part of the conversation, the man calmed down and actually affirmed several people on the team. It seems he was upset and angry because he was afraid he was going to be blamed again for a less than stellar result, but when he felt heard and understood, his fear evaporated. By the end of the meeting, everyone had agreed on a plan, each had a specific responsibility, and our timeline was set.

If I had tried to ignore the man's angry outburst, he probably would have become even more upset, he would have assumed the worst about me and the others on the team, and trust would have been seriously eroded. If I had blasted back and put him in his place, the others on the team might have felt vindicated…but they also might have wondered if they were going to be my next targets. Using the obvious tension as a starting point for honest conversation provided a safe place for everyone to calm down, value each other, and find a process so we could move forward.

USING OBVIOUS TENSION AS A STARTING POINT FOR HONEST CONVERSATION PROVIDES A SAFE PLACE FOR EVERYONE TO CALM DOWN, VALUE EACH OTHER, AND FIND A PROCESS TO MOVE FORWARD.

AVOID THE EXTREMES

We make a huge mistake when we demonize tension...and the person whose face represents it. When it's a threat, we automatically retreat to *either/or* thinking: a person is either a good guy or a bad guy, not a complex guy; in a relationship, we're either all in or all out, not realizing human connections are sometimes difficult but valuable; and situations are either wonderful or terrible, not good or not so good and needing improvement. The more insecure we feel, the more we'll look for simple, clear answers. The problem, of course, is that many of the most valuable things in life aren't so simple. Certainly, there's objective truth, but the Bible says we need wisdom to discern not the good from the bad, but the good from the better.

Attempts to completely eliminate tension actually create more tension, for us and the people around us. Oversimplifying keeps us from seeing the beautiful complexity of life, and it pigeonholes people instead of seeing them as multidimensional and infinitely interesting.

And if we insist on seeing others as all good or all bad, we probably see ourselves the same way, which produces arrogance or shame. We overlook our own faults or we're consumed with them. Either way, we're hypersensitive to criticism—and even a mild question about our motives or decisions—which blocks our growth and makes us like porcupines. People are afraid to get too close or they'll get stuck!

When we live in the extremes, we're always on guard and we can't relax. The constant tension gradually erodes our resources and distorts our outlook. We become unhealthy emotionally, physically, financially, and relationally. To compensate, we may try to act like nothing bothers us, or we may become fiercely competitive and insist we're right about everything.

Businesses and organizations have to face the reality of conflicting objectives. These tensions can't be completely resolved, so the leaders must decide which objectives require the most attention at any given point. A *Harvard Business Review* article by Dominic Dodd and

Ken Favaro identifies three common pairs of competing objectives in business:

1. Profitability versus growth
2. Short-term versus long-term
3. Whole versus parts

In churches and nonprofits, the tensions are somewhat different: personal growth of constituents versus numeric growth of the organization replaces profitability versus growth, but the other two are essentially the same. Every organization has to invest in the future at the same time they focus on present performance, and leaders have to coordinate all parts of the company, church, or nonprofit while they give attention to the effectiveness of each component part. Dodd and Favaro conducted a three-year study and concluded that many corporate leaders don't even recognize these tensions, and when they do, they often focus on the wrong one at any given time. When their attention is riveted on one, they may ignore the importance of the others. And each one requires a different, but related approach. The authors explain:

> Because the three tensions interact…it is difficult to disentangle cause from effect and problem from symptom. But despite the close relationships among them, each tension raises different questions and prompts managers to take a different focus. The tension between profitability and growth focuses the leader on the company's *business model:* what it does for customers and how it configures its costs to support that. In other words, it prompts questions of strategy. The tension between the short term and long term requires that leaders examine the company's *management model:* how the company manages performance and investment. It prompts managers to think about the company's targets, processes, and routines. The tension between the whole versus the parts steers leaders toward considering the company's *organizational model:* its structure, culture, and people. This means that managers need to carefully think through their companies' problems to make a diagnosis.[21]

In life and in leadership, we need to grasp the complexities we face each day. We face competing choices, and they're seldom written in black and white. Almost always, they're in shades of gray. As we make choices, we'll realize that every *yes* is pregnant with many *no*'s. In business, these are called *opportunity costs* because a choice necessarily eliminates other opportunities. We want to go to two different places for a vacation...we have two wedding invitations for the same day...we've received two job offers...there are two movies playing that look attractive.... When we pick one, we eliminate all of the rest.

When Jesus was about to launch the greatest enterprise the world has ever known, He met with His closest followers in the upper room. This meeting was electric with tension—tension with the disciples who were arguing about who would be the greatest in Jesus's coming kingdom, tensions with Judas, tensions with Peter, and Jesus's tensions within Himself as He faced the excruciating future of going to the cross. Jesus's response to all of this wasn't to run away or bark condemnation at those who didn't appreciate what He was going to do. Instead, He took off His cloak, wrapped a towel around himself, picked up a basin of water, and washed their feet. In the middle of the most profound and searing tension anyone had ever faced or would ever face, Jesus embraced the moment and took the role of the lowest servant.

> **AS WE MAKE CHOICES, EVERY YES IS PREGNANT WITH MANY NO'S. IN BUSINESS, THESE ARE CALLED OPPORTUNITY COSTS BECAUSE A CHOICE NECESSARILY ELIMINATES OTHER OPPORTUNITIES.**

Later that night, He experienced tension when Peter, James, and John couldn't stay awake with Him as He poured out His heart in prayer. He was completely in charge of the moment when Judas betrayed Him with a kiss and Peter cut the ear off the high priest's servant. Jesus spoke calmly and clearly in the mock trials and in front of the Roman governor who claimed to have power over Him. And He endured the greatest imaginable tension when the Father withdrew so He could bear the punishment for the sins of the world. Jesus knew that these tensions were temporary but His mission was eternal. He refused to get distracted from the Father's purpose. He certainly didn't ignore the stress and tension He faced, but He kept His eyes on a far bigger goal than relief.

Jesus had a choice to live in tension and stay in the Father's plan or escape it by calling twelve legions of angels to slay His enemies and rid Him of the pain and shame of the cross. I'm glad He stayed.

We have choices, too. We can let tension destroy us, or we can invite it to strengthen us. What will we choose?

JESUS KNEW THAT HIS TENSIONS WERE TEMPORARY BUT HIS MISSION WAS ETERNAL. HE REFUSED TO GET DISTRACTED FROM THE FATHER'S PURPOSE.

THINK ABOUT IT:

1. What are some consequences in our thoughts, our moods, and our relationships when we insist on trying to get rid of all tension?

2. Review the many ways tension can destroy us. Which ones have you seen in your life or the lives of others?

3. Review the ways tension can strengthen us. How have you seen people, including yourself, grow through facing tension with courage?

4. In what ways does simplistic thinking feel right but lead to emotional, physical, financial, and relational problems? Why, then, does it look so attractive?

5. Why is it important for leaders of businesses, churches, and other organizations to notice the three most common organizational tensions and find ways to address them?

6. How is Jesus's example of facing the reality of tension a model for you?

APPLY IT:

+ As you read this chapter, what tensions described here reminded you of your experiences?

+ How did you respond at the time?

+ How do you want to respond next time?

+ Who do you know who is experiencing a similar tension today?

+ How can you help this person embrace the tension, resolve the tension, or use the tension to stimulate an innovative solution?

5

TENSIONS IN IMPLEMENTATION

What man actually needs is not a tensionless state but rather
the striving and struggling for a worthwhile goal,
a freely chosen task. What he needs is not the discharge
of tension at any cost but the call of a potential meaning
waiting to be fulfilled by him.
—Viktor Frankl[22]

Before I became the president of a college, I was a pastor, and as you
may recall, I could count the people in the pews on that first Sunday, not

counting family members, on two hands...and have a finger left over. Delegation wasn't really something I needed to think about because every responsibility fell on *my* shoulders. As the church grew, my solution was to make better and longer lists, talk faster, drive faster, and do more in every minute of the day. I was in charge of leading, speaking, visiting, planning, scheduling, implementation, quality control, and the outcome. I was a one-man band. When I was named the college president, I immediately applied my consummate pastoral management skills—I tried to do everything myself. Soon, though, I realized this wasn't going to work. I had to find a way to trust others, involve them in the process, and give up a large measure of control to talented, dedicated men and women.

At the time, the college was in trouble. Enrollment was down... and declining even more. We had difficulty retaining the best people on our staff and the future looked bleak. Maintaining the status quo was leading us in the wrong direction. For the situation to change, *I* had to change. I had to grow into the job and I had to make monumental progress—really fast!

I understood that maintaining complete control had its benefits, but the liabilities were far greater. If I tried to lead the college the same way I'd led the church, I would be a bottleneck that choked off the life-giving stimulation of others' creative ideas and efforts. I decided to create an executive team. It seems like an obvious solution, but for me at that stage of my leadership development, it was a very large leap. I asked five people to join me on the team.

Immediately, we ran into two problems: I didn't know how to delegate and they didn't know how to respond to delegated authority. Each of them had demonstrated skill in their areas of responsibility, but they had functioned like the CEOs of their five departments, with very little communication and virtually no coordination. Now, I was asking them to come together to support each other, stimulate each other, and coordinate programs with others on the team.

In addition to the other challenges we faced, we needed to jump through the academic hoops to apply for accreditation. I delegated the feasibility study to one of the people on the team. I delegated the planning for our development campaign to another person and asked him to research the potential donor base. We considered adding another field of study; I asked another team member to study the possibility and come back with a plan for focus groups and a new curriculum.

The college's executive team was my classroom in learning to delegate. Sometimes, I did well, but occasionally (at least I'd like to think it was only occasionally), I bombed. I had to learn who on the team was creative and could fill in the blanks...and who needed very specific direction. When I was a pastor, I made changes on the fly, but now I had to figure out how to get objective feedback at each phase of a program so we could make any necessary midcourse adjustments. Identifying incremental benchmarks was a new idea for me, but this concept proved to be incredibly helpful. And of course, I had to confront people on the team when they didn't do what they had been assigned, didn't do it well enough, or delayed getting it done. When I was a pastor and a one-man show, the finger always pointed at me. Now, I had to learn to be both direct and kind as I pointed out how someone could do better the next time.

Sometime during that first year as the college president, I understood that good delegation doesn't begin with the people on the team; it begins with me. I had to understand them, I had to communicate clearly, I had to blend the vision and the specific steps of implementation, I had to stick to the timeline, and I had to shepherd talented and opinionated people throughout the process.

MANY OF THE BEST LEADERS ARE VISIONARIES; THEY CONCEIVE A NEW REALITY OUT OF A HOST OF UNKNOWNS.

The learning curve of implementing plans through delegation was steep for me. The lessons I learned in that pivotal year have continued to be refined over the decades. Today, they're a vital part of my conversations as I meet with leaders in business and the church. Leaders face a number of tensions as they take steps to see a vision become a reality.

ABSTRACT AND CONCRETE

Many of the best leaders I know are visionaries; they conceive a new reality out of a host of unknowns. They're abstract thinkers, but most of the people on their teams are far more concrete. These leaders inspire their congregations and employees with a new vision of the future, but they often leave their teams frustrated—and these are the people who work the closest with them and have to carry out their plans. Staff members and top employees want to know *who does what by when*; if they don't have those specific, clear instructions, they become immobilized or frantic, guessing what they're supposed to do, but sometimes stepping on the toes of other members of the team who are also playing the guessing game.

The problem is that few people on the team are intuitive enough to figure things out and create concrete steps out of the abstract picture. Sometimes, only one team member is that astute. The leader looks at that person and thinks, *Why can't everybody be like her?* In reality, most people aren't wired that way. They're gifted, they're eager and motivated, and they have experience and expertise, but they need clear tracks to run on. If the leader doesn't provide them, they're all in trouble.

In addition, visionary leaders are usually more than a few steps ahead of everyone else, and they don't want to get bogged down in the nitty gritty of detailed planning, fine-tuning, reporting, and midcourse corrections. But the people on the team *need* this kind of input, as well as plenty of encouragement for the tangible progress they're making along the way. Implementing an idea is much more than the leader articulating a glowing image of what can be; it requires the details of planning, delegation, and feedback that are essential to success.

It's certainly possible for visionary leaders to provide concrete direction. I've seen some outstanding leaders slow down to identify the plans and phases of a large program. They give specific benchmarks for each phase to their teams and all of their constituents so they'll know when they're on target and on schedule; when some area has proven to be unrealistic and needs rethinking; and what kind of adjustments need to be made. But leaders who excel in both worlds, abstract and concrete, are rare. That's why many large churches now have executive teams who play this role, and businesses have chief operating officers and other top executives who provide concrete steps for the employees so the vision can become a reality.

LEADERS NEED TO ACQUIRE THE SKILL—AND THE PATIENCE—TO EQUIP EVERY PERSON ON THE TEAM TO FEEL CONFIDENT AS THEY CARRY OUT THEIR RESPONSIBILITIES.

It's important for leaders to envision the future. Their abstract thinking has gotten them into their leadership roles, but they need to acquire the skill—and the patience—to equip every person on the team, no matter how concrete their thinking may be, to feel confident as they carry out their responsibilities. When leaders take time to provide clear direction and answers, they create a stable, encouraging, innovative environment where everyone can thrive.

Delegating is more than moving a task from one person's to-do list to another's. That's dumping. Delegating is giving responsibility and authority to someone who can do the job as well as you, or who can learn to do it as well as you—or even better than you. This implies respect for the person's intelligence, expertise, and commitment to the goals of the team.

Those who are skilled at the art of delegation ask good questions on the front end. When we wait to ask questions after the person has failed, they come across as condemning instead of helpful. For any significant task or program, we need to take the time to ask people:

- Who can help you accomplish this?
- What will it look like when it's done?
- Does the timeline work for you?
- What resources do you need?
- What are your benchmarks of progress?
- What do you need from me?

> **LEADERS SHOULD LET THEIR TEAM MEMBERS KNOW THEY ARE AVAILABLE. SAY, "I'M MORE THAN GLAD TO HELP IN ANY WAY, BUT I WANT YOU TO COMMUNICATE CLEARLY AND OFTEN WITH ME ALL ALONG THE WAY."**

I ask people to give me a heads up if they're running behind schedule. Of course, this request instills fear in people who don't want to tell the boss they're not getting the job done, so I make sure to tell them I'll only be upset if they *don't* tell me about a delay. I often say, "Consider me your primary resource. I'm more than glad to help in any way, but I want you to communicate clearly and often with me all along the way."

Know yourself and know your people. It's wonderful to have a person or two on your team who can think in abstract terms and can fill in the blanks of a global and sketchy vision, but don't assume everyone is like that—or that everyone *should be* like that. Tailor your communication to the concrete people on the team. Everyone will be glad you did.

INTUITION AND ADVICE

Some leaders are so intuitive that they have a feel for what needs to happen long before anyone else has a clue. That can be a great strength or a tragic weakness. When people on their teams believe their input doesn't matter, they feel devalued and their motivation wanes. Intuition is one of the most important traits of leadership, but *many leaders don't know what they don't know.* Instead of relying on their gut feeling, they need to invite input from others who have proven to be insightful and reliable.

When I was the college president, I started the habit of saying to our executive team, "I have an idea. It's not final by any means, so I need your help to make it better." When I then shared the idea, everyone felt free to give input to shape it into something we all believed in. I didn't say, "Here's my idea. We're not going to change it at all. I only want you to implement it." When I asked them to make it better, I was saying that I was coming up with a concept, and I was committed to it, but I needed their involvement to make it what it could be. The idea itself wasn't up for debate, but the form, the timing, the people involved, and all the nuances were in wet cement until our team tackled these issues.

Instincts are primal and God-given, but *intuition* can be acquired. We can develop the skill of anticipating future opportunities and challenges, but we usually need help. I know very effective leaders who have put themselves in relationships with talented men and women, and these mentors and friends asked tons of questions to find out what makes the leaders tick. These rising leaders are voracious readers, studying their field, going to conferences, finding a mentor or coach, and listening to podcasts. Gradually, they develop a sense of what works and what doesn't, who to trust and who not to trust, how things can be improved and what can be a drag on productivity, what motivates each person on the team and what undermines their enthusiasm and energy. By the time most of us become leaders, we've developed our intuition about our role—but the best leaders never stop reaching and learning. Their intuition continues to be refined over a lifetime.

Some leaders are on the other end of the confidence continuum. They don't seem to be able to make decisions until they've squeezed the last drop of advice from everyone they know. And even then, they believe they need more input before they can take a step. They second-guess themselves; they're always looking over their shoulders, wondering who will catch them making another mistake.

ALL OF US—IN BUSINESSES, CHURCHES, AND FAMILIES— LIVE IN THE TENSION BETWEEN INTUITION AND ADVICE.

All of us—on teams in businesses and churches, as well as in families—live in the tension between intuition and advice. I've gone into meetings with my team with a strong sense of what we need to do and how we need to do it, but the counsel around the table completely changed my mind. They gave me new information, they gave me a different slant on information I already had, or they reminded me of other priorities that would have to be shelved or delayed if we proceeded on the course I was suggesting. I entered the meeting with a resounding, "Yes, we've got to do that!" but I left saying, "I'm so glad we're not going to do that!" (And of course, this happens all the time in my relationship with Brenda!)

To embrace the tension, we value our gut feelings, but we remain open to others as they contribute their ideas to shape the concept or communicate concerns that reroute it. Assuming our intuition is always right is arrogant and foolish. It kills a lot of great ideas from the people around us and it robs them of the belief that they matter. On the other hand, people who seldom trust their gut are like balloons blowing in the wind. Every person's opinion has the power to change their minds. This, too, results in frustration among people on the team and in the family.

The starting point is important. I start with my intuition and then invite others to give their input, but plenty of spouses and leaders begin with a wet finger in the air to gauge the direction of the wind. Only then, when they know they won't be challenged, do they promote an idea...

and even then, they're susceptible to the shock of new information or people changing their minds.

ASSUMPTIONS FORMED EARLY

Our most basic assumptions about life didn't drop from the sky. They were formed in our childhoods as we watched how our parents and siblings responded to us and each other. If we saw the most important people in our lives drift to either of the ends of the continuum of living by intuition or being afraid of their intuition, we may emulate them or take the opposite track. Since opposites attract, many couples have one of both: perhaps the wife is very intuitive and the husband wants everyone to sign on to an idea before voicing a conviction. The tendency isn't a fatal flaw as long as each spouse values the other's bent. But it becomes a frequent friction point when they resent each other's leaning and blame each other for being compulsive or indecisive.

None of us arrives at adulthood as a whiteboard. The handwriting of our parents—and sometimes aunts, uncles, grandparents, and siblings—is all over our mental maps. We've internalized the words, tone, presence, actions, and attitudes of our parents. We may copy one of them, or we may go the other direction because we've been so deeply hurt, but the impact of this relationship is deep and lasting.

In an article for *Entrepreneur*, Jeff Haden identifies the tension between intuition and advice. Communication, he asserts, must be a two-way street:

Business is filled with what: What to execute, what to implement, what to say, and sometimes even what to feel. What's often missing is the why. That's why so many projects, processes, and tasks fail. Tell me what to do and I'll try to do it; tell me why, help me understand why, help me believe and make that why my mission too…and I'll run through proverbial brick walls to do the impossible. Managers stipulate. Outstanding leaders explain. And then they listen—because the most effective communication involves way more listening than talking.[23]

Haden says the very best leaders are aware that they need help. As they rise in authority and responsibility, they may be tempted to display an air of superiority, but that can be a fatal flaw. He reminds us:

Outstanding leaders don't pretend to know everything. (In fact, they purposely hire people who know more than they do.) So they instinctively ask questions. They automatically ask for help. And in the process they show vulnerability, respect for the knowledge and skills of others, and a willingness to listen—all of which are qualities of outstanding leaders.[24]

Playing it safe certainly reduces risk (and embarrassment), but it crushes creativity and severely reduces the thrills life can offer. If no one ever wonders if you've lost your mind, you may need to push a little more toward trusting your gut. In an article for *Inc.*, Sunny Bonnell describes the necessity for leaders to move beyond the zone of safety, but even then, it's tempered by reason and input:

When you act on your gut, you're unpredictable. Mercurial. Authentic. You make leaps of logic and see connections others miss. Gut instinct lets you see beyond where your business is today to what it could be tomorrow. That's why it's such an important part of what I call the Rare Breed. Don't get me wrong—instinct isn't always right. Brain science tells us that useful gut instinct depends on having plenty of knowledge and experience about your field. And as powerful as intuition is, if you don't follow it with planning, skill and strong management, all you've got is a cool idea on a whiteboard.[25]

TO LIVE IN THE TENSION, WE FIRST NEED TO UNDERSTAND WHICH SIDE OF THE CONTINUUM WE USUALLY LIVE, AS WELL AS ITS BENEFITS AND LIMITATIONS.

To live in the tension, we first need to understand which side of the continuum we usually live. We can recognize the benefits of being there, but also the limitations. Those who are intuitive can learn to ask for input, but they can also be more vulnerable when they're wrong and praise others who give good advice. And those who seldom move without consensus or unanimity can take more time before meetings to pay attention to their gut. Both can embrace the other side—at least a little—and be better leaders, spouses, and parents.

TIME INVESTED AND TIME SPENT

To use our banking analogy again, there's nothing wrong with spending money on things that are valuable, but if we're spending without generating revenue from investments, we'll run out of money. Or in this case, we run low on time and influence. Some leaders refuse to delegate because they insist, "I can get the job done quicker and better if I do it myself." If that's true, it's a leadership failure. That's *spending* our time and resources instead of *investing* them in the people on our teams to equip them to be as effective as ourselves. Our reluctance to delegate limits the range of available resources to our own talents and time, reduces the scope to what can be accomplished by one person, and demoralizes the people around us who are eager to contribute but feel ignored.

OUR RELUCTANCE TO DELEGATE LIMITS THE RANGE OF AVAILABLE RESOURCES TO OUR OWN TALENTS AND TIME, REDUCES THE SCOPE TO WHAT CAN BE ACCOMPLISHED, AND DEMORALIZES THE PEOPLE AROUND US.

When I spend time with friends, I never consider that time to be wasted. It's important—crucial, in fact—to enjoy one another. To make the time meaningful, we don't have to accomplish anything beyond understanding each other's hopes and fears and having some laughs. But in other relationships, I invest my time to build up the people around me. Some will become better leaders, some will become more talented in a specific skill, and both sets of people will have a greater impact.

LEADERS WHO INVEST WISELY...

HAVE A PLAN OF WHAT THEY WANT TO DELEGATE.

We tailor our assignments to each person's talents, interests, and capacity to develop them for future responsibilities.

CHOOSE COMPETENT, PASSIONATE PEOPLE.

Far too often, I've seen leaders pour themselves into people who either didn't care or weren't ready. Investors look for the best return they can get, so they carefully analyze stocks, bonds, real estate, and other financial opportunities to find the right ones. In the same way, we need to be wise in selecting the people in whom we invest our time and wisdom.

CLARIFY EXPECTATIONS.

When our input is scattered and unclear, people feel frustrated. Our goal isn't just for us to speak plainly about what we expect; we don't stop communicating until the person can articulate the expectations as well as we can.

DEFINE AUTHORITY AND RESOURCES.

It's unfair to give responsibility without authority, and it's discouraging (and confusing) to assign tasks without providing the resources needed to succeed. An essential step, then, is to make sure the person has a clear grasp of the delegated authority—that is, the range of decision-making—and how to acquire everything necessary to fulfill the responsibility.

FOLLOW UP TO ENCOURAGE AND MAKE ADJUSTMENTS.

People thrive on affirmation…and they die without it. When great leaders delegate, they stay involved—not hovering over the person, but staying in contact to receive updates. This gives the leader plenty of opportunities to praise the person and, if necessary, to give input for adjustments. Without this involvement, leaders are often caught off guard by problems no one told them about. This, of course, creates the wrong kind of tension in the relationship!

CELEBRATE OTHERS' SUCCESSES AS MUCH AS THEIR OWN.

When an investor reads the balance statement and realizes his money has made a lot more, he's thrilled. When a leader sees the success of the people on the team, he realizes his investment has paid huge dividends. He's not threatened by others' success. Instead, he now views their success as the primary measure of his own success.

LEADERS WHO INVEST POORLY…

DON'T DELEGATE—OR DO SO THOUGHTLESSLY.

Such leaders don't delegate, don't delegate clearly, or they dump responsibilities on their people to get those things off their plate. Failures in delegating authority and responsibility waste time, are inefficient, and fail to develop people. Everyone is exasperated.

DELEGATE TOO QUICKLY OR TOO SLOWLY.

One confuses and the other frustrates. Good leaders develop a rhythm so people on the team know what's expected of them, know how to process information, and feel confident that the due dates are reasonable.

WITHHOLD AUTHORITY AND RESOURCES.

Poor leaders put up obstacles so their people will have trouble accomplishing their tasks. These leaders may withhold authority because they want to retain it all, and they may limit resources because they don't really want the person to succeed. When the person is struggling, the leader can ride to the rescue and look like a hero...to everyone but the people who know what really happened.

ARE THREATENED BY THE SUCCESS OF OTHERS.

Leaders who are so insecure that they sabotage others' efforts create a toxic environment. In these situations, many people on their teams see self-preservation as their primary goal. They jockey for positions, blame each other, and form alliances, all of which ruins the chemistry of the team.

POTENTIAL AND PROBLEMS

Investments are long-term ventures. We don't measure the wisdom of an investment by what happens today or tomorrow, but by what happens in the future. The best investors see potential where others see problems. When I served as college president, the janitor on our campus was Benson Karanja. In my conversations with him, I could tell he was a remarkable man. As a result, I opened door after door for him to receive educational and career opportunities, and he excelled in them all. At one point, I asked him to join our executive team, and then I promoted him to be my executive vice president. I met with him before our meetings to talk about the agenda and my goals for each item; we met after the meetings to talk about what had happened. I could say, "Here's what you saw, but here's what was really going on." I believed in him, so I was glad to invest my time and attention in him. When I left the college, Dr. Karanja became my successor as president.

Who has invested in you? Who saw talents to be developed and character to be refined, and considered you worth the time and attention to help you take steps forward? These people saw alignment between your goals and theirs, so they had confidence that your progress would advance their agenda.

Delegation is much more than moving work from our page to someone else's page. It's an opportunity to develop them, stretch them to try something new, test them to see if they're ready for more responsibilities, and promote them when they're ready. Wise, attentive delegation creates a pathway for people to excel.

> **WISE, ATTENTIVE DELEGATION CREATES A PATHWAY FOR PEOPLE TO EXCEL.**

A FEW OR MANY

Many leaders spend time with too many people and fail to invest time in those who can make the most difference in their company, church, or nonprofit. It's certainly not wrong to spend time with plenty of people; that's a part of being visible and communicating the message of the organization. But investing in a few multiplies the leader's impact. Jesus spoke to the masses, but He invested most of His time on the twelve apostles and His inner circle was the trio of Peter, James, and John. They were the ones who saw His most intimate moments, undoubtedly had the opportunity to ask more poignant questions, and received the greatest opportunities to see into His heart.

For you, who are the many...and who are the few? Who are the people around you who *need* your investment, who *want* your investment, and who will thrive as leaders *because* of your investment?

I've seen that many leaders don't mentor a few because they've never been mentored; they delegate poorly because they've been under leaders who didn't know how to empower and believe in the people around them. These leaders already feel stretched because of the many demands of their role and they see mentoring a few people on their teams as one demand too many.

It's amazing what happens when leaders reorient their priorities to build into the lives of a few people. Yes, some adjustments to their schedule need to happen so they can have coffee with this person every week or lunch with that one. But over the months and years, believing in that person will usually bear enormous amounts of fruit—in the person's effectiveness, the leader's sense of fulfillment, and the organization's growth.

All leaders live in the tension between the few and the many. Most of them need to move more decisively toward a few.

IT'S AMAZING WHAT HAPPENS WHEN LEADERS REORIENT THEIR PRIORITIES TO BUILD INTO THE LIVES OF A FEW PEOPLE.

NOW AND THEN

Leaders are often future oriented, and many have risen to their position because they're demanding and driven. These traits are valuable to raise the bar for everyone involved in the organization, but too much focus on the future can leave people feeling empty and discouraged today. I believe celebration is a vital part of a leader's agenda, but far too often, we wait much too long to enjoy success. I've known many leaders who waited to celebrate until after the last nail was hammered in the new building, the last dollar was raised, and the last day of a long program had arrived—and that's much too long. By then, many people are so exhausted that the only ones who are thrilled are those who haven't worked so hard to see it completed. Instead, leaders can combine the concept of benchmarks of progress with genuine celebrations of success all along the way. Great leaders are experts at celebrating incremental successes.

We've all heard the old saying about longevity in marriage: "Those who pray together stay together." But for teams, those who *play* together stay together. When the members of a team can relax and enjoy each other outside their normal routine and responsibilities, they learn things about each other they would never have known by sitting side by side in hundreds of staff meetings.

FOR TEAMS, THOSE WHO PLAY TOGETHER STAY TOGETHER.

Playing together on a regular basis isn't time wasted; it's time invested in the health of the team. These moments, including times of celebrating progress toward a goal, increase the level of trust, lower defensiveness, provide energy, and promote longevity because people feel valued and want to stay on the team.

I tell leaders to put a line item on their agendas and budgets: fun. It's that important, and it won't happen unless it's planned. Contrary to what you might think, this is time invested, not spent, in the emotional health of the team. On these outings, they don't need a devotional message or prayer. They can go to a ball game, have a picnic, attend a concert, go to the zoo, play games, or do all of these at different times. I know one leader who has a *Director of Ambiance*, someone in charge of finding plenty of options for fun times with the team. That's not this person's only job, but it's an important one.

I recall an old commercial for motor oil. The spokesman stood next to a car with the hood raised so we could see the engine, and he said, "You can pay me now or pay me later." He meant that people could change their oil at very little expense, but if they waited too long, their engine problems would incur far greater costs. It's the same with leadership. Many leaders spend far too much time and emotional energy correcting the problems of poor delegation. If they invested more on the front end, building relationships through fun and delegating thoroughly, they'd save themselves and their teams a world of headaches. Certainly, delegating well at the beginning may take more time than doing the tasks themselves, but developing a larger group of talented, enthusiastic people will produce big returns in the future.

> **WHEN LEADERS BUILD RELATIONSHIPS THROUGH FUN AND DELEGATE THOROUGHLY, THEY SAVE THEMSELVES AND THEIR TEAMS A WORLD OF HEADACHES.**

Why do many leaders fail to delegate well? As we've seen, there may be many reasons, but the one I've noticed most often is that they're preoccupied with all the things they need to do, so they don't give clear directions when they delegate. For every task assigned to anyone on the team, we can ask the simple, but wonderfully comprehensive question: "*Who* does *what* by *when?*" If all three of those components are clear from the beginning, more will be accomplished, frustrations will be minimized, and misunderstandings virtually eliminated.

To visionaries, the details of delegation can seem incredibly dull and boring, but they're absolutely necessary for the team to be effective and for everyone to be excited about their assigned tasks. Successful implementation isn't a mystery. It takes forethought, investment in a few, and plenty of celebration.

THINK ABOUT IT:

1. Where are you on the continuum of depending on intuition and seeking advice? Where on it are the people closest to you? Does the difference cause any friction? Explain your answer.

2. Describe the impact of the people who have invested in you over the years.

3. What principles of delegation do you already do well? What ones need some improvement?

4. Who are *the few* you're investing in or want to invest in? Why them? What does progress look like in each of these relationships?

5. Why are having fun and regular celebrations so important to the emotional health and productivity of a team or family?

6. What are some of the benefits of investing time and energy on the front end of delegation instead of on the back end when you see problems?

APPLY IT:

+   What tensions mentioned in this chapter reminded you of your own experiences?

+   How did you respond at the time?

+   How do you want to respond next time?

+   Who do you know who is experiencing a similar tension today?

+   How can you help this person embrace the tension, resolve the tension, or use the tension to stimulate an innovative solution?

6

TENSIONS WITH THE VISION

The greater the tension, the greater is the potential.
—Carl Jung

A few years ago, I consulted with a prominent pastor who had planned to build a much larger worship center, but he hadn't anticipated some monumental challenges. At first, everything looked like green lights. They had a carefully considered architectural plan, there was plenty of enthusiasm on the part of the staff, and the building committee had allocated funds to get the project off the ground. Liftoff was imminent.

But soon it appeared that the planning hadn't been quite as comprehensive as I'd been told. The funds available weren't enough to convince the bank that the project was feasible, so the bank officer turned them down. The second bank came to the same conclusion, as did the next four banks. Each one explained that the available funds weren't enough to qualify for the loan being sought. When the church raised more money, the bank officers said, they'd be glad to talk to them again.

The problem was that the vision had already been cast and people were excited to see it happen. Their enthusiasm then crashed on the hard rocks of reality. Over the next five years, the pastor went back again and again to the top donors, asking for more money. He didn't have great news to share with the staff, so he tried to avoid the topic whenever possible. When people in the congregation asked staff members for updates, they either deflected the conversation to a different topic, or shrugged their shoulders—responses that didn't exactly inspire confidence! The grand plans to reach more people and provide more programs for the community faded away. The pastor kept telling the congregation that they were "almost ready" to start construction, but after a while, no one believed him. The church experienced vision fatigue, the donors experienced request fatigue, the staff experienced confusion fatigue, and the people didn't know what in the world was going on.

When the pastor's level of chronic disappointment surpassed his vision for the future, he too lost hope that the building would ever be constructed. He second-guessed himself and the Lord. Maybe he hadn't really heard from God…maybe the vision was for the next pastor, but not him…or maybe he hadn't tried hard enough yet. The donors—and by now, this group included virtually everyone at the church—had given money to the project, but they hadn't seen any progress. The pastor felt trapped: he couldn't move forward unless he raised even more money, and he certainly couldn't give up on the project and tell people their money had gone for nothing. And that's when he called to ask me to consult with him.

Another pastor who asked me to consult with him is the greatest idea generator I've ever known. He has more ideas in a day than most of us have in a year, or maybe a lifetime. A few of his concepts have enough staying power to remain on his agenda for a month, but most of them vanish when the sun goes down. His staff quickly learned that they couldn't take action on anything he said because he would have a new and different idea the next day. For a long time, many of them tried to find ways to plan and secure the resources to implement some of the ideas. They asked good questions to make sure a project aligned with the church's vision and values, and they discussed the phases of progress. However, the pastor quickly got bored with this level of conversation; his body language told them he had disconnected from them. His credibility plummeted as their eyes glazed a few minutes into every meeting. His mind generated innovative concepts, but his actions produced lethargy in his staff.

WHEN A LEADER CAN'T LAND ON A CONCEPT LONG ENOUGH TO BRING IT TO COMPLETION, EVERYONE COMES TO THE CONCLUSION THAT IT'S NOT WORTH THEIR TIME TO EVEN TRY.

There's nothing wrong with a leader changing his or her mind. That's part of the discovery process for any idea. But when a leader can't land on a concept long enough to bring it to completion, everyone around him comes to the conclusion that it's not worth their time to even try. A few staff members and top employees become so demoralized, they give up and leave, but many drift off to their own spheres of responsibility and do the best they can. They pour themselves into their work, but they suffer from the nagging truth that they're less effective because they can't coordinate their efforts very well with the others on the team.

Families can have a vision, but it's usually more intuitive than articulated. They have unspoken but very real values and a culture that has been reinforced from generation to generation. Most families genuinely celebrate each other's successes, which shows that their chief value is the flourishing of each person. A few families go through the process to craft a family vision, often about passing a business from parents to children, or perhaps to train each generation to serve passionately and selflessly. I want the members of my family to experience God's blessings of good health, strong and enduring relationships, and a purpose bigger than ourselves. If we impart these values and vision, I'll be thrilled.

HISTORY AND HORIZONS

To lead any kind of genuine change, we have to live in the tension between the lessons we've internalized in the past and the path to new horizons. Past success is not the best predictor of future success. What we *already know* can get in the way of what we *need to know* as we think about taking the next steps.

Genetic testing and the Internet have made researching family history a modern phenomenon. Some of us are obsessed with finding out who we are and where we've come from. This research has made it possible to discover far more about our backgrounds than we've known before—even more than Aunt Mable wrote in her long letter to your mom! We discover more than an abstract family tree; we uncover stories about our ancestors that thrill us, amaze us, or would embarrass us if we'd lived closer to their time. When we go back to identify the people in our families and learn more about their stories, we have the opportunity to grasp what made our grandparents and parents the way they were. This gives us more understanding, perhaps more empathy, and almost certainly more appreciation for all they endured to carve their lives out of hardships and adventures. We have the chance to reframe this history, not to change it, but to reinterpret it in a more positive, even heroic, light.[26]

IN EVERY ROLE AND RELATIONSHIP, WE NEED TO KEEP AN EYE ON WHAT HAPPENED YESTERDAY SO WE'LL HAVE CONTEXT FOR TODAY AND WE'LL UNDERSTAND THE OPPORTUNITIES FOR TOMORROW.

In every role and relationship, we need to keep an eye on what happened yesterday so we'll have context for today and we'll understand the opportunities for tomorrow. For instance, in a marriage, some people wonder why their spouse continues to react in the same way to the same annoyances. If we explore a little bit, it's not that hard to figure out: the past history of the relationship definitely shapes responses today, and quite often, the history of the spouse's relationship with his or her parents colors present reactions. The pattern is usually thoroughly predictable, but only if we step back, open our eyes, and see the patterns of history. Then we can understand how to chart a path to a better horizon.

FLOW, SYSTEMS, AND STRUCTURE

A *system* is an organizational chart created to accomplish all the tasks of the business or church; it becomes a *structure* when names are put in the slots and specific responsibilities are assigned. *Flow* is the leader's innate sense of what needs to happen and who can do it. A number of the leaders I know have remarkable intuition—they sometimes can't explain why they believe their organization needs to take a specific step; they just know it. But I also know leaders who have carefully constructed a workable system and have recruited, trained, and placed very competent people for each position. I believe the best leaders live in the tension between flow on one side and systems and structure on the other.

Problems arise (and multiply) when leaders are weighted too much on one side or the other. All flow and weak systems leave people wondering what they're doing, why they're doing it, what's most important, and when things need to be done. Frustration and chaos are the inevitable results. On the other hand, leaders who rely too heavily on their systems and structure have the benefit of predictability in everything they do, but they miss out on the adventure of spontaneity. Their people often feel like cogs in the leader's machine—doing their jobs but without passion and purpose.

It's wise to create long-range plans—five, ten, or even twenty years—but life happens, and leaders need to be nimble enough to catch a wave of opportunities they hadn't foreseen. Some types of companies are almost constantly in flow. Logistics, communication, social media, and transportation are in perpetual change. For them, the planning horizon is seldom longer than a year, or even a few months, because technology is changing their business models so fast. Who would have dreamed ten years ago that we'd be seeing driverless cars and trucks on the highway? I consult with a business owner who is pioneering an innovative type of aircraft. What will people think of next? This is precisely the point.

Leaders who value flow take advantage of opportunities that seem to appear out of nowhere. They're looking for waves in their industry or the culture, and they make adjustments. They train their people that being flexible is part of their job description, and they shouldn't be surprised when they're asked to change priorities, learn new skills, and find new ways to get new jobs done.

ALL STRATEGIC PLANS SHOULD BE WRITTEN IN PENCIL. IT'S IMPORTANT TO KEEP OUR EYES OPEN TO NEW OPPORTUNITIES.

All strategic plans should be written in pencil. The organizations that are too rigid miss opportunities, are often confused when they fall behind, and need to find someone to blame. Planning certainly is necessary, but it's important to keep our eyes open to new opportunities.

When I was a college president, I quickly discovered that academia is perhaps the field most deeply entrenched in systems and structures and the least willing to change. But we decided to change the system: we began to offer courses to nontraditional students who were in their forties, and those who already had careers and families. To accommodate their schedules, we held classes at night. We also proposed sweeping changes in financial aid, professors' schedules, and the ways students interact with each other so they would be stimulated to apply what they were learning. All of these changes seemed perfectly reasonable to us, but the accrediting body reacted like we had thrown a hand grenade into their reserved, antiquated academic world! When they challenged our plans and our goals, we answered all of their questions, and we were successful in making the adjustments to our new system. The results were instantly encouraging: many people who assumed they had no chance to get a higher education found the doors open to them.

In many marriages, one person is flow and the other structure; one has creative ideas and the other thinks them through to create workable plans; one incurs the bills and the other pays the bills. The difference can create resentment...or it can produce a beautiful blend if each one learns to appreciate the other.

I see the tension between flow and systems and structure as a river. The current of the water is the creative flow, but without the banks of systems and structure, it floods the surrounding houses. And the banks without the flow would be meaningless, barren, and dry. One isn't better than the other. They only work when they work together. If someone only values flow, they find systems and structure to be severely restrictive instead of directional and necessary. And if someone is dedicated only to systems and structure, the spontaneity of innovation is missing, and the river is shallow and stagnant.

At different stages of an organization's or a family's life, the tension between flow and systems and structure can change. For instance, leaders of startup companies and church plants spend a lot of time planning their launch, but they usually soon discover they didn't anticipate some of the challenges or the surprises of unique opportunities. The first years are full of adjustments as they fine-tune their systems to take advantage of the flow. But if their systems become calcified, they'll miss the next wave of opportunities that comes to them. In families, the years of starting a family add many unknowns. Some people thrive in the chaos, but many desperately need some sense of order so they can retain their sanity. As the kids grow up and leave, and as finances aren't quite as tight, they can relax more, loosen their schedules, and enjoy more spur-of-the-moment activities.

Today, we can find hundreds (maybe thousands) of books and seminars on the importance of finding balance in our lives. I've come to the conclusion that this goal doesn't adequately address reality. Life comes in spurts. For many of us, the requirements of job or family mean that we devote a lot of time, at least for a while, to these responsibilities. At various points, though, we find space to breathe, to recharge our engines, and to enjoy things we neglected during the pressurized times. If we tried to balance each day during all of this time, we'd be very frustrated and probably confused, but if we realize the ebb and flow of life, we may not find the perfect balance in each day, but we'll find the right rhythm. Problems arise when we don't find relief from times of intense responsibilities. Difficulties also surface when we feel guilty because we assume we should be able to find balance every day, or others try to make us feel guilty because we aren't spending the same amount of time every day doing what they think we should be doing.

PROBLEMS ARISE WHEN WE DON'T FIND RELIEF FROM TIMES OF INTENSE RESPONSIBILITIES.

In our organizations, we need to embrace the tension between flow and systems and structure; in our personal lives, we seek rhythm instead of balance.

OLD AND NEW SYSTEMS

The history of organizations is littered with companies that failed to revise their systems when times changed. Old systems are what used to work; new systems are the ones needed to flourish now and in the future. The company's vision is the driving purpose, and the system is the vehicle that takes you there. If you have a finely crafted vision but an antiquated vehicle, you'll be stuck on the side of the road as your competitors rush past you.

I believe we can identify a powerful cycle of organizational success[27] from vision to dominion:

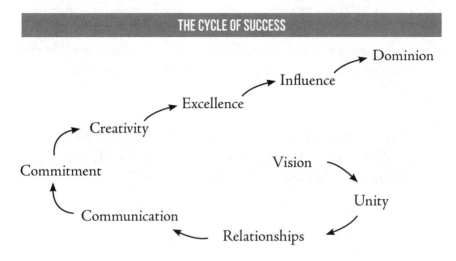

THE CYCLE OF SUCCESS

- ✦ *Vision* produces unity because it invites everyone to participate in a purpose greater than themselves. The vision describes the what, the how, and the when.

- ✦ *Unity* deepens relationships—the who.

- ✦ *Relationships* enable clear communication.

- ✦ *Communication* reinforces shared commitments.

- ✦ Shared *commitments* create an environment of creativity.

- ✦ *Creativity* results in excellence.

- ✦ *Excellence* increases influence.

- ✦ And as influence grows, the organization can have *dominion* in the field.

Dominion isn't necessarily exclusive presence, and it doesn't imply brutalizing the competition, but it means the organization commands respect, has a significant market share, and is a leader in innovation. Certain airlines have had dominion in particular regions around the world, Amazon is the dominating force in marketing and sales across the globe, and some churches have a far greater impact on their communities than any others. These organizations weren't satisfied with old systems, so they created new ones to take advantage of opportunities. However, they didn't completely throw out the old. They lived in the tension between what has worked well, what wouldn't work in the future, and the new systems required to take big steps forward.

> **DOMINANT ORGANIZATIONS LIVE IN THE TENSION BETWEEN WHAT HAS WORKED WELL, WHAT WOULDN'T WORK IN THE FUTURE, AND NEW SYSTEMS REQUIRED TO TAKE BIG STEPS FORWARD.**

RISK AND SAFETY

In 1955, Ford Motor Company decided to produce their first new car in a decade. They conducted extensive research and found that the post-war economic boom would enable them to sell up to 400,000 of the new line of cars each year. They looked at models the other major car companies were producing, and they were sure their innovative design would be a winner. They named it after the company owner's son, Edsel Ford. However, by the time the first Edsels rolled off the assembly line in 1957, the market had changed, and sales were far less than projected. The experiment lasted only two years. *Time* magazine reported:

> As it turned out, the Edsel was a classic case of the wrong car for the wrong market at the wrong time. It was also a prime example of the limitations of market research, with its "depth interviews" and "motivational" mumbo-jumbo. On the research, Ford had an airtight case for a new medium-priced car to compete with Chrysler's Dodge and DeSoto, General Motors' Pontiac, Oldsmobile and Buick.... The flaw in all the research was that by 1957, when Edsel appeared, the bloom was gone

from the medium-priced field, and a new boom was starting in the compact field, an area the Edsel research had overlooked completely.[28]

The last Edsel was produced in 1959. The confidence of Ford's executives was shaken and they didn't introduce another car until 1964, when they rolled out the first Mustang, one of the most popular cars of all time.

People have always been fascinated with leaders who are willing to risk it all. In the last quarter of the nineteenth century, John D. Rockefeller took over the new oil and gas industry and dominated it for decades. As the country rapidly grew, Andrew Carnegie was a lion in the steel industry. Today, Jeff Bezos, Oprah Winfrey, Steve Jobs, Richard Branson, and Elon Musk are household names because they dared greatly...and won their bets.

We're going to make mistakes when we try to live in the tension between risk and safety—it's guaranteed. If we wait until success is 100 percent sure, it's too late because others will have jumped in and captured the idea and the market. And if we're afraid to lose, we won't take chances. On the other hand, if we don't take time to do enough research and jump in without thinking it through, we may leave a wake of shattered dreams (and shattered trust) behind us.

In an article for *Inc.*, Minda Zetlin quotes a successful CEO who describes "5 Things the Smartest Leaders Know about Risk-Taking." They include:

1. "Any risk should serve your company's mission."

   An adrenaline rush isn't enough reason to take risks. They should be strategic, carefully considered, and in alignment with the organization's vision, values, and goals.

2. "You really have to be OK with failure and losses."

   Leaders who can't live with failure—and haven't learned how to use failure to teach lessons to everyone on the team—will be frozen and unable to try anything new.

3. "It's perfectly fine *not* to take risks."

It's foolish to take unnecessary risks, ones that aren't in alignment with the company's vision, ones that don't fit the timing of other plans, and ones that will cost too much if they fail.

4. "Risk-taking comes with a cost."

Many risks in companies and churches stretch finances, which cause leaders to shift allocations away from other areas, such as hiring, infrastructure, or other resources.

5. "It can take a very long time for risky endeavors to pay off."[29]

It's almost guaranteed that the return on investment for risky ventures takes longer than the leader expected.

This is a tension we live with all our lives. Every time we drive a car or ride in one, or we choose a restaurant, vacation destination, clothes, or a financial investment, we intuitively weigh the risk and the need for safety. Some of us need a gentle push to be a little more adventurous and some need to put on the brakes a bit more. If we know ourselves and we get good feedback from people who understand our tendencies, we'll learn to live more effectively in this tension.

> **SOME OF US NEED A GENTLE PUSH TO BE A LITTLE MORE ADVENTUROUS AND SOME NEED TO PUT ON THE BRAKES A BIT MORE.**

NOW AND NEXT

The effective life cycle of a church is about twenty-five years. If the leaders don't reinvent themselves and relaunch the church, they'll become stale and stagnant. From what I've seen:

+ In the first three to five years, the church is establishing its identity. The leaders encounter their first major conflict, often about direction, resources, and programs. The leader may lose some people and finances, but the rebound is usually quick and complete.

+ In about years eight through ten, the church suffers a second significant conflict, but this time, it's about people. This is often a *me or them* moment for the pastor: "Either they go, or I go." For instance, a staff member who functioned adequately when the church was smaller can't handle the increased responsibility that comes with growth. Everyone likes her and she has developed a strong network of people who believe in her. Moving her to another role—or if she becomes defiant, removing her from the team—causes a destructive ripple effect throughout the church. Or the conflict may be with one or more people on the board whose support has turned to opposition. Whatever the source of the disturbance, this is a time of severe testing. In this stage, the pastor must make some hard decisions; he needs to invest time and energy into making sure the right people are in the right roles.

+ During years eleven through thirteen, the church has significant momentum and the programs are largely successful. The church is growing and everyone is optimistic about the future. However, in this stage, the pastor often has second thoughts about himself—thoughts the rest of the staff and the church would never guess he has. Growth in the church causes him to assess whether he wants to continue in the primary role as shepherd or if he believes God wants him to become more of a CEO. This can be a very difficult time in the private life of a pastor, even as everything visible is going exceptionally well. If he chooses to change roles, his responsibilities shift, priorities change, and relationships are affected. At this point, the pastor has a choice: he may engage in self-reinvention, bring in highly competent people, clarify goals and roles, and chart a path to greater growth, or he may realize the cost is too high to make massive changes, so he backs away from any grand dreams.

After all, the church is growing, people are happy with the current direction, and it's not worth the pain a new direction would inflict. Instead of pulling the church into congruence with his new vision, he gives up on the dream and becomes congruent with the existing vision. It's not necessarily cowardice at all; in fact, it may be the epitome of wisdom. If he chooses to implement the sweeping new vision, he and the church will pay a price. The strain of this stage causes many to leave—and if the new direction produces too much friction, the pastor may be one of those out the door.

+ As the church nears the twenty-five-year mark, it may encounter a perfect storm of exhaustion, growth beyond the capacity of the staff, financial struggles, and perhaps a transition of leadership. The pastor may be bored now with what has been successful for the previous decade or so, and he wants to do something new, different, and bold. He believes he has an abundance of leadership equity, and he assumes everyone will gladly go along with his new vision. He may be right and stay to lead a thriving church until he retires. Or he may be wrong, in which case the church implodes around him as hurt feelings multiply into accusations and exits.

Before this crucial point at year twenty-five, the leader and the leadership team need to do some soul searching and evaluate virtually everything they are, everything they've been, and everything they hope to become. Hard decisions need to be made. I consult with the pastor of a church that is nearing its thirtieth anniversary. He's in this evaluation process now. He and his leadership team have been in a long process of reinventing and relaunching the church with renewed vision, a streamlined staff team, younger members on the leadership team, and some young leaders who bring energy and the willingness to take bold risks.

Companies may go through a similar cycle of launch, growth, conflict, stagnation, and relaunch, but instead of twenty-five years, the complete cycle is probably closer to twelve or fifteen. The speed of a church's life cycle is affected by competition with other churches in the community, but businesses have far more numerous and aggressive competitors. For example, the kind of plastic used for bottled water was developed in 1973. This enabled companies to bottle and sell different versions of water. Four decades later, the annual consumption of bottled water in America was 9.67 billion gallons, an average of almost 31 gallons per person.[30] By one count, at least 132 companies have at least one brand of bottled water, and they fiercely compete in the market to sell every drop. Each company has to regularly find ways to relaunch their brand to excite customers. And what are they buying? Water—just water.

A number of authors have identified five stages in the lifecycle of businesses. I've adapted the ones listed and described by Neil Petch, chairman of Virtugroup, in an article for *Entrepreneur*:

1. Concept

In this stage, the entrepreneur studies the market, the viability of a product or service, and the feasibility of making a profit in a reasonable period of time.

2. Startup

Those who launch new businesses often make the mistake of undercapitalizing their companies, so they don't have adequate funding in this crucial stage. Also, they have to adapt quickly when they discover they have a bigger opportunity than they realized or what they're offering isn't as attractive as they had imagined.

3. Growth

By this point, most of the bugs have been worked out, systems are working, people are functioning, and the company is making money. There's a sense of relief, blended with excitement about the future.

4. Expansion

New products, new markets, and new people propel the company forward to more profits and impact. In this stage, planning is as important as ever, even though things seem to be already going smoothly.

5. Decline, Exit, or Relaunch

Missed opportunities and exhaustion can lead to a gradual decline in the company's viability, or perhaps an economic downturn causes a precipitous and catastrophic decline in sales. If the company is still thriving, the owners may decide to sell and move on, or perhaps to find renewed energy and relaunch the company with new products, vision, and passion.[31]

Families experience cycles and may encounter major changes in a very short time, propelled by an unexpected and severe illness, an untimely death, graduation, marriage, promotion, loss of employment, a move to another community, or any of dozens of other factors. At home, at work, and in church, we live in the tension between now and next. Each stage has its own opportunities, and we can be sure that we'll face new challenges as time and situations change.

Some people thrive on change, but many feel threatened by it. Stability is valuable...until it becomes the primary goal of a church, a business, or a family. A vision is a fragile thing. It can easily be eroded by fear or doubt, it can be shattered by failure and betrayal, or it can stand the test of time and motivate people to accomplish more than they ever imagined. These tensions are very real. Wise leaders recognize them, live in them, and help their people embrace them.

THINK ABOUT IT:

1. How does a person's history hold them back or propel them forward? How has your family history affected you? How does it continue to affect you?

2. In your organization, how would you describe the tension between spontaneous flow and its systems and structures? Are you happy with this blend? Why or why not?

3. Why is a *balanced schedule* not a reasonable goal? What is?

4. What aspects of the old system still work and will take your organization into the future? How would new systems (or at least significant adjustments in the old one) be beneficial?

5. Do you lean toward taking risks or playing it safe? Do you need to make any adjustments in your risk tolerance? Explain your answer.

6. Why is it important to understand the stages of a church, a business, or a family?

APPLY IT:

+ As you read this chapter, what tensions described here reminded you of your experiences?

+ How did you respond at the time?

+ How do you want to respond next time?

+ Who do you know who is experiencing a similar tension today?

+ How can you help this person embrace the tension, resolve the tension, or use the tension to stimulate an innovative solution?

7

TENSIONS WHEN FACING HARD CHOICES

The tension between what is, and what we dream of, is important. Not to discount what we have, but to hold onto that middle ground, because it's in there that the magic happens.
—Susan Branch

I met with a pastor of a large and growing church. He had called me because he felt overwhelmed and didn't know what to do. After we talked several times and I observed his leadership, I told him, "I'm impressed with how the church has grown under your leadership, but you're running it like it's about three hundred people."

He looked at me like I'd said I was from outer space, so I thought I'd better explain. "You still want to be involved in every decision, you go to every meeting, and it doesn't appear that you've distinguished between the tasks you must retain and those you need to delegate. With the size of your church, the number of things you need to keep on your list of priorities should be fairly limited, but right now, it seems limitless."

He looked stunned, but he also finally was able to clear away the fog that had confused him for a long time. He asked, "What's the first thing I need to do?"

I responded, "Think of yourself as the CEO."

"And then?"

I smiled. "Then you need to reorganize everything to be sure you delegate well, and you'll retain control over how things are run. You're still the spiritual leader of the church, but the way you manage the systems will be very different. You'll have clear metrics of growth, you'll have an effective reporting system, your meetings will be more focused, and you'll probably need to make some staff changes because some responsibilities will shift from you to them. Very soon, you'll know who your stars are and who your utility players are. You'll focus on developing relationships with people who believe in your vision and will become financial backers. You'll identify the 20 percent of your people who give 80 percent of the donations, and you'll identify the 5 percent who give 50 percent."

I could see the wheels were turning in his mind. I decided that was enough, so I told him, "That's your second step...and for now, it's your last step." We both had a good laugh. Over the next several months, we had wonderful conversations about the many and very difficult decisions he was making during the transition. It wasn't just a transition for him; it was also a major shift for his leadership team. And they made it. The pastor made courageous decisions to move some people on his team into new roles, hire new people, create new systems, communicate well and often, and calm the fears of many who were afraid they wouldn't have a place any longer. Soon, he felt comfortable in his new, dual role of shepherd and CEO, and his team had confidence in him and themselves in their redefined responsibilities. The church continued to grow, most of the staff members rose to the challenge, and the pastor no longer felt overwhelmed.

STARTUPS AND GROWTH

As we've seen, we experience tensions in every field, every relationship, and every stage of life. One of the seasons when leaders feel inordinate amounts of tension is after startups, in business or in churches. The initial vision and the launch generate enough adrenaline to power a small city, but every entrepreneur faces important choices that leave an impact—for better or worse—for years to come. And these choices often make or break the venture itself.

In business, the statistics are staggering. Founders rarely become successful CEOs over the long haul of their company's life. The traits that prompted them to conceptualize and launch the company aren't the same ones needed to develop it into a stable venture. In "The Founder's Dilemma" in *Harvard Business Review*, Noam Wasserman reported his research on startup companies:

> Every would-be entrepreneur wants to be a Bill Gates, a Phil Knight, or an Anita Roddick, each of whom founded a large company and led it for many years. However, successful CEO-cum-founders are a very rare breed. When I analyzed 212 American start-ups that sprang up in the late 1990s and early 2000s, I discovered that most founders surrendered management control long before their companies went public. By the time the ventures were three years old, 50% of founders were no longer the CEO; in year four, only 40% were still in the corner office; and fewer than 25% led their companies' initial public offerings. Other researchers have subsequently found similar

trends in various industries and in other time periods. We remember the handful of founder-CEOs in corporate America, but they're the exceptions to the rule.[32]

Wasserman found that four out of five entrepreneurs are forced to step down because investors insist on someone with better management skills. Before that fateful day, the founders usually assumed the investors believed in them and were loyal to them, so most are shocked at this demand. The founders' resistance is echoed among the employees they have brought in, who have much more faith in them than in the investors.

Almost without exception, founders face very difficult choices soon after their company is launched. They have to decide if their primary goal is to make money for themselves, or to lead a successful company. If they want to be rich, they can strike a deal with the investors and walk away with considerable cash; if they want to lead a successful company, they have to determine what role they fit best...and often, it's not as the CEO. Either way, the emotional connection to the initial idea of the product, the first forays into the market, the hiring of enthusiastic people, and the investment of long hours cause the founders to believe the company is *their baby*. The tension with the investors can be intense and ugly. Founders believe they've earned trust by giving everything they've got to make the new company a success, but the investors have a cold eye on profits—and feelings are expendable. They insist on better systems, more skilled division leaders, and better financial management. The investors also often demand the power to control who is on the board, including the selection of the chairman. In all of these decisions, the entrepreneur can feel pushed aside, often because he *is* pushed aside!

Entrepreneurs eventually have to make the hard choice between riches and control. If they define success by staying in the top position, they may retain control at the sacrifice of losing some investors. If they give in to investors' demands for a new leader, they may come away with more money in their pockets, but perhaps with the disappointment that someone else is now in charge. Or that may have been the entrepreneurs' plan all along.

Church planters are a different breed from the rest of us. Like founders in the business world, they have an idea, a dream, and usually a small group of people who have bought into their vision. Instead of angel investors, they may be backed by their home church, their denomination, a church-planting organization, or their families—and quite often, a combination of these sources. Relatively few church planters have participated in launching churches before. They have friends who have done it, they've visited churches that are new plants, and they've been to seminars, but actually doing it is new to them.

> **LIKE FOUNDERS IN THE BUSINESS WORLD, CHURCH PLANTERS HAVE AN IDEA, A DREAM, AND USUALLY A SMALL GROUP OF PEOPLE WHO HAVE BOUGHT INTO THEIR VISION.**

FOUR STAGES OF COMPETENCE

Five decades ago, management trainer Martin M. Broadwell identified "the four levels of teaching."[33] A few years later, Paul R. Curtiss and Phillip W. Warren used Broadwell's model in *The Dynamics of Life Skills Coaching*. We can apply the four stages of competence for the leader of a church launch:

1. UNCONSCIOUS INCOMPETENCE

They don't know what they don't know. Arrogance or assumptions (or both) create enormous headaches, even from the start.

2. CONSCIOUS INCOMPETENCE

As the startup pastor studies and learns, he begins to realize the full scope of what he doesn't know. The wise leader understands that he has a lot to learn, and he's a sponge soaking up all the information he can find.

3. CONSCIOUS COMPETENCE

The church planter has gained knowledge, refined his skills, and recruited some talented people who are both enthusiastic and realistic. The leader and the team are ruthlessly honest about the task before them, and they're determined to gather all the necessary resources to make it work.

4. UNCONSCIOUS COMPETENCE

With enough experience and the wisdom that comes from success and failure, launching and leading a new church becomes second nature to some church planters. This person becomes a valuable resource to others who are eager to learn.[34]

PASTOR AND CEO

As we've seen, as churches grow, pastors have another hard choice: to continue to be a shepherd to everyone in the church or transition to a different leadership style as a CEO. The vision doesn't change, and the core values aren't diluted, but the pastor's concept of his role shifts to become a visionary leader. The change affects how meetings are conducted, who is in these meetings, how the leadership team is structured, the criteria for hiring and promotion, and the process of decision-making. These changes usually surprise some, thrill others, and cause concern among many who wonder what the shift means for them. In fact, the one who may wonder more than any others may be the pastor. He has served diligently and well for many years with a particular concept of his role, so he feels uncomfortable—and he may even feel it's wrong!—for even considering this shift in style and identity.

Churches can grow to about 250 or 300 people with the pastor in the role of the shepherd, but to grow beyond that point, the transition must take place. This means, of course, that the role of shepherding will be shared with others on the team. The lead pastor will still shepherd some of the people in the church, but as the church grows, he can't provide personal care for everyone. When the church was small, shepherding may have taken up to half of the pastor's time, but as it grows, much more of his time will be invested in the typical work of a CEO: studying options, providing direction, casting vision, creating culture, making major decisions, providing resources, and following up to make sure progress is on schedule.

As I've consulted with pastors over many years, I've watched some of them struggle with the dual roles. I've explained to them that they'll still be a pastor when they add the role of CEO, and they have to be both at the same time. At any given point, one is their priority over the other—and it can get complicated. To the paid staff, they are primarily the CEO who leads them in the business management of the church. However, when a staff member or a lay leader in the church has a personal need, they function as a pastor. Church members view them as primarily their pastor and secondarily as the church CEO. This is a crucial distinction: if the pastor gets this wrong, he'll put projects before people. If he sees people primarily as a means to accomplish his projects, he'll use them instead of nurturing them; he'll threaten, push, or flatter them to manipulate them to fulfill his agenda. Sooner or later (and often sooner) the people he leads become polarized—for him or against him. This, I believe, is the source of a lot of tension in churches today. The change to a workable dual role may be necessary, but it isn't easy or quick. It needs to be approached with wisdom and humility.[35]

The change, however, comes with some risks. If a pastor functions primarily as a CEO, he may put projects in front of people and treat them as cogs in the accelerating machine. When this happens, people feel used and manipulated, believing the pastor's strong statements are threatening and his affirming words are no more than flattery. Trust is built as leaders serve first as pastors and then as CEOs.

COMPASSION IS A VALUABLE TRAIT, BUT IT SHOULDN'T CLOUD OUR THINKING AND ACTIONS ABOUT SOMEONE WHOSE ATTITUDE IS POISONING THE TEAM.

The distinction is important for all paid staff of the church because they realize they were hired for what they know and what they can do, but they may be fired for who they are. In other words, attitude is everything. Too often, I've seen senior pastors switch from their role as a CEO who needs to fire someone to revert to being the pastor who gives the employee a second chance… and often a third and a fourth and…. Compassion is a valuable trait, but it shouldn't cloud our thinking and actions about someone whose attitude is poisoning the team. Our care can be demonstrated in how we help them make the necessary transition off the team.

When I look at Luke's account of the early church in the book of Acts in the Bible, I see a number of CEO decisions by the apostles. On the day of Pentecost, they cast a big vision, and soon they organized people into groups to care for their needs. When their system didn't work and the widows from a Greek background felt overlooked, the apostles didn't bury their heads in the sand. They looked at the problem, realized their system didn't fit the need, changed it, and recruited the right people to lead. As the church grew and was dispersed by opposition, they moved the headquarters from Jerusalem to Antioch. (See Acts 11:19–26.) Jerusalem was the center of religious life for the Jews and the new group of Christians, but Antioch was a commercial center. From there, trade radiated out across the empire; from there, the gospel could radiate to the same places. The apostles were responding to Jesus's commission to go to all nations, not just to the Jews in Palestine.

After Paul met Jesus on the road to Damascus and spent a few years preparing for his role as a church leader, he and Barnabas launched their first missionary journey. When they returned, they had startling news: Gentiles had become Christians! Some of the church leaders insisted that these Gentiles convert to Judaism and follow the Law to be Christians. (See Acts 15.) It was, as one sociologist observed, the first great crisis in church history. If James and the Jerusalem counsel determined that people had to become Jews to become Christians, the new movement would remain only an offshoot of Judaism. But if they determined that faith in Christ was all the Gentiles needed to be full members of the body of Christ, the movement could expand exponentially. Acting as a de facto CEO, James spoke up, making the hard choice to go against the very fervent and vocal leaders who opposed him…and the church grew among the Gentiles. Most of us reading this book are part of the Christian church because of this monumental decision.

A few years later, Paul blended his theological, pastoral, and CEO skills to plant churches, help them grow, and multiply leadership throughout the Roman world. In Philippi, he first met with Lydia, a wealthy woman in the business world. (See Acts 16.) The next person Paul encountered was a slave girl who was possessed by a demon. Paul cast the demon out, and her owners were outraged. In the subsequent melee, Paul and his companion Silas were arrested and thrown into the deepest part of the dungeon, where they were put in stocks. As they sang praises that night, God caused an earthquake to break their chains and open the cell doors throughout the prison. The jailer was ready to commit suicide in shame over letting the prisoners escape, but Paul stopped him and led him and his family to Christ. The church in Philippi began with a wealthy businesswoman, a freed slave girl, and a jailer's family…and later, Paul wrote his most endearing letter to thank them for their support. (See Philippians.) In every city where Paul planted churches, the leaders were encouraged to be both pastors and CEOs. When we read his letters to the churches and to Titus and Timothy, we see this powerful blend of roles.

MAJOR AND MINOR DECISIONS

"All men are created equal"—but our decisions aren't. We make countless decisions every day, and many are so automatic that we don't even think about them. But if we analyze our lifetime of choices, most of us can identify a few monumental decisions that have determined the quality and direction of our lives. I have four: immigrating to the United States in 1973; marrying Brenda in 1979; leaving the pastorate to become a college president in 1989; and leaving the college in 2003 to become a full-time leadership consultant. These four decisions are infinitely more significant than what I'll have for breakfast tomorrow,

which shirt I choose to wear, the route I'll take in traffic, and all the countless other decisions I've made or will make today. Whatever I choose in those may be tastier, make me look better, or make me late or on time, but they won't affect my life in any material way.

The principle of the relative magnitude in decisions applies in every area of life. In meetings, a leader and the team often address twenty or more decisions, but usually, one or two are far more important than the rest. The decision where to build a house is *the* decision; the color of the living room is *one of countless* decisions. Selecting the architect or the plans is *the* decision; the company that hangs drywall is one of many.

> **THE ITEMS ON AN AGENDA ARE MORE THAN JUST A CHECKLIST. TIME SPENT ON THEM SHOULD BE BASED ON WHETHER THEY ARE HIGH, MEDIUM, OR LOW PRIORITIES.**

Business and church leaders need to figure out what are the most important decisions in every meeting they have with staff teams, boards, and strategic planning committees. If all of the decisions seem to be equally important, they won't devote enough attention to the few that deserve more study and thought. Many of us view the items on an agenda as just a checklist. As long as we can put a check next to each one, they all look the same. But there's a big difference between the two or three most important decisions and the rest. It's wise to at least put a star next to those before the meeting so you'll be sure you spend plenty of time on them. In fact, I recommend three categories of importance: high, medium, and low. And if you don't get to a few that are in the low category on the list of priorities, you can put them back on the list the next week.

What are the characteristics of those two or three decisions? When I look at the list of agenda items, I instinctively ask two questions:

1.   Which decisions have a sustainable impact? In other words, what are the long-term implications?

2.   Which ones have breadth and depth of impact?

Most of the decisions on the agenda, I quickly realize, don't measure up to these criteria. It's not that they're irrelevant, but they don't need equal attention with the ones that are high priority. Good leaders focus on the things that are most important. They may assign some decisions to their staff and ask for a report the next week. Everything doesn't have to be decided at the top level of leadership.

WHEN WE SEE ALL DECISIONS AS EQUAL, WE UNDERVALUE THE PRIMARY DECISIONS AND WE OVERVALUE ALL THE SECONDARY ONES.

When we see all decisions as equal—and maybe the easy ones as more important because checking them off gives us a quick *win*—we undervalue the *primary* decisions and we overvalue all the secondary ones. We also fail to do due diligence to discover the points that help us make the right decisions on the most important ones.

Making this distinction, of course, is a way to train everyone on the team to prioritize a few decisions over others. They have team meetings, too, and they will be better leaders if they focus on what's most important. And then, those people will train the people they lead.

One of the factors that shapes the priorities of at least some leaders isn't the answer to the two questions I posed earlier. Their chief concern is how people will react to the decision, and they change their minds based on the response of the team. That's following, not leading.

At the college when I was president, *the* decision was to focus our attention on adult students. This led to many subsequent decisions, such as changing the configuration of classrooms and replacing desks with tables and cushioned chairs to promote comfort and collaboration, initiating night classes, and instituting block scheduling so students could come to the college only a few nights a week instead of every night. By accident, soon after we implemented the changes, I realized that virtually every student now drove to campus and met during a three-hour timeframe in the evening, so our limited parking spaces weren't sufficient. I discovered this reality when I drove in one night and couldn't find a place to park. The decision to focus on adult students had a sustainable, wide, and deep impact.

The corporate landscape is littered with companies that didn't identify and answer the most important questions. Blockbuster made the transition from VHS to DVD, but they didn't make the switch to streaming movies. When Netflix and Amazon made their play for the market, Blockbuster was left behind. Dell was the darling of the computer world, but only for a while. They innovated by selling directly to customers, but they failed to realize mobile devices were the new wave in technology, and they didn't enter the new world. Eastman Kodak cornered the market on cameras, and they developed brand awareness with their color film and Instamatic cameras. However, when digital cameras became the rage in the 1980s, Kodak's business model became obsolete. Sears, Toys "R" Us, and other brick-and-mortar stores are being hammered by online retailers. The ones who jumped into the online market are competing with the giant, Amazon, but the rest are either struggling or giving up. In each case, the company's leaders either saw the trends but didn't make the right decision, or they didn't see the choice in the first place.

Today, many couples get married with an implied escape clause: if things get tough, the not-so-tough will get going! In a marriage, *the* decision is to stay married. Then, when they hit rough patches, they're not looking for a way out; they're looking for a way back up. They also have key decisions about how they'll spend, save, and invest; how they'll raise their children; where they'll live; how to prioritize work; and how they'll relate to in-laws. For Brenda and me, one of the most important choices we made was that we were going to work hard to teach our daughters the skills of decision-making.

The tension between big and little decisions is one most of us don't think about, but if we do, we'll spend more time making sure we get the big ones right.

OBVIOUS AND OBLIVIOUS

Has your spouse ever given you *that look* at a dinner party or business function, delicately motioning that you have a piece of spinach in your teeth or a bread crumb on your lip? And you thought people were staring at you because you have such a winning personality! The spinach or the crumb was obvious to her (and everyone else at the table), but you were oblivious to it.

Actually, the shoe can fit on either foot. Sometimes, we're the only ones who can't see something that's obvious to everyone else, but occasionally, others are oblivious to what's obvious to us. One person may be more observant than another, or at a deeper level, she may be more perceptive and be able to *read* others. For some, this remarkable trait is simply a God-given talent, but others may have suffered verbal, physical, emotional, or sexual abuse, and have become *hyper-vigilant* to notice every tone of voice, every gesture, and every movement of body language as a defense against being hurt again.

I've known people who are incredibly perceptive about systems and processes, but they don't have a clue what inspires and discourages people on their teams. And I've known plenty of people who are wonderfully insightful about people, but their eyes glaze over when I talk about reporting structures, communication systems, and decision-making processes.

As leaders and parents, we often see realities our followers and children don't see. Many of us get frustrated and mutter under our breath, "Why don't they see it? It's so obvious!" The simple fact is that we have been where they are at some time in the past...and maybe not that long ago. And no matter how far we've come, there are still a lot of things we don't see, we don't understand, and we don't perceive. This fact gives us a healthy dose of humility…and patience. We conclude that their inability to see what we see doesn't make them bad people, or even deficient people. We're just a little farther along in our maturity and have honed our skills of perception a little more. Our value isn't wrapped up in what we know and see, and their value isn't diminished by their limitations in what they know and see.

In His most famous sermon, Jesus gave an illustration that must have made people laugh. It was about perception and our tendency to harshly condemn others:

> *Why do you look at the speck of sawdust in your brother's eye and pay no attention to the plank in your own eye? How can you say to your brother, "Let me take the speck out of your eye," when all the time there is a plank in your own eye? You hypocrite, first take the plank out of your own eye, and then you will see clearly to remove the speck from your brother's eye.*   (Matthew 7:3–5)

Imagine the scene of this illustration: a friend has a tiny speck of sawdust in his eye. He's squinting and rubbing his eye. You want to take it out, but you have a fence post sticking out of your eye! You can't see a thing. Jesus says, "Wake up! Realize your own problems with perception before you run in to correct the sight of others!" This means that I should be more concerned about my pride, my inflated self-confidence, and my lofty estimation of my talents than the limitations of those around me. Humility is a rare and beautiful thing. The hard choice is to wade in and admit our own flaws, our own pettiness, and our own lack of love—but that's exactly what's required. Then and only then will we have the kindness and gentleness to take the speck out of someone else's eye.

OUR VALUE ISN'T WRAPPED UP IN WHAT WE KNOW AND SEE, AND THEIR VALUE ISN'T DIMINISHED BY THEIR LIMITATIONS IN WHAT THEY KNOW AND SEE.

LEADING AND SERVING

Organizational expert Tom Peters said the formula for success is simple: "Organizations exist to serve. Period. Leaders live to serve. Period."[36] In the last few decades, we've heard a lot about *servant leadership*. This concept will never become obsolete. Every person in a leadership position lives in the tension between leading (being out front and challenging people to reach higher) and developing (being alongside to help people take their next steps). The same blend of roles is found in the term *visionary shepherd*. Almost a half a century ago, Robert Greenleaf coined the term *servant leader*. He wrote:

> The servant-leader is servant first.... It begins with the natural feeling that one wants to serve, to serve first. Then conscious choice brings one to aspire to lead. That person is sharply different from one who is leader first, perhaps because of the need to assuage an unusual power drive or to acquire material possessions.... The leader-first and the servant-first are two extreme types. Between them there are shadings and blends that are part of the infinite variety of human nature.
>
> The difference manifests itself in the care taken by the servant-first to make sure that other people's highest priority needs are being served. The best test, and difficult to administer, is: Do those served grow as persons? Do they, while being served, become healthier, wiser, freer, more autonomous, more likely themselves to become servants? And, what is the effect on the least privileged in society? Will they benefit or at least not be further deprived?
>
> A servant-leader focuses primarily on the growth and well-being of people and the communities to which they belong. While traditional leadership generally involves the accumulation and exercise of power by one at the "top of the pyramid," servant leadership is different. The servant-leader shares power, puts the needs of others first and helps people develop and perform as highly as possible.[37]

Leaders who don't wrestle with this tension are either too far out in front and don't bother to come back to help those who are following, or they're not out in front at all. Those who are called to lead in businesses, churches, and families need a clear, compelling vision of the future, coupled with compassion for those who are taking halting steps to keep up with them.

> THOSE WHO ARE CALLED TO LEAD NEED A CLEAR, COMPELLING VISION OF THE FUTURE, COUPLED WITH COMPASSION FOR THOSE WHO ARE TAKING HALTING STEPS TO KEEP UP WITH THEM.

We face a wide range of difficult choices. We can try to escape these tensions by insisting they don't exist or by leaning too far in one way or the other. The best leaders, though, learn to be comfortable living in ambiguity, providing clarity where they can and comfort when they can't.

THINK ABOUT IT:

1.   What are the tensions between the energy and courage to start a business or church and the tenacity to keep reaching and growing?

2.   If you're a leader in a church, how would you describe the difference in roles of a pastor and a CEO? When, if ever, is it good and right to make this transition?

3.   What are the four or five most significant decisions you've made in your life? How would your life be different if you'd made other choices each time?

4.   Do people consider you to be a perceptive person? Explain your answer. (And ask your spouse!)

5.   Who do you know who best exemplifies a servant leader? What are this person's qualities and impact on others?

APPLY IT:

+   As you read this chapter, what tensions described here reminded you of your experiences?

+   How did you respond at the time?

+   How do you want to respond next time?

+   Who do you know who is experiencing a similar tension today?

+   How can you help this person embrace the tension, resolve the tension, or use the tension to stimulate an innovative solution?

8

TENSIONS IN COMMUNICATION

A good listener is not only popular everywhere,
but after a while he knows something.
—Wilson Mizner

A pastor and his leadership team asked me to meet with them because they were considering some sweeping changes and they didn't want to make any big mistakes. The church was twenty-eight years old. The demographics of the surrounding community had become much more diverse, significantly younger, and more secular. The church's services and programs were virtually unchanged for more than twenty years, and many of the people in the congregation looked like they had been original members. The pastor realized his church was becoming increasingly irrelevant in the community.

Over the previous decade, the pastor had instituted a few changes, but people from the outside wouldn't have noticed any difference; in fact, many of the people in the church didn't want to see any difference! People who attended for the first time felt like they had entered a scene from *Back to the Future*. If they wore jeans and had tattoos, they received more sideways stares than warm handshakes. It was apparent that the back door was as wide as the front door, and very few young people stuck around more than a week or two.

When I met with the pastor and his team, they shared their vision and their plan to change the culture of the church, implement sweeping changes, and reach the people who had been turned off by the church in recent years. Actually, I met with several teams led by members of the executive team, and each one had an excellent plan. Together, their ideas and direction formed one of the most promising plans I'd ever seen in a church. I told them I was very impressed, and then I asked them how they were going to communicate their plans. The pastor and his team looked at me like I'd spoken to them in an ancient Middle Eastern language. "Well," the pastor slowly began, "I'm not sure what you mean. We're going to share the vision and the plan with the congregation. That's pretty obvious, isn't it?"

"Not really," I answered. For the rest of our meeting, I explained a communication strategy. It was something they'd never heard before, and obviously, they'd never imagined.

BROADCAST AND CASCADE

The pastor's office had a whiteboard. I took a marker and began drawing a pyramid with several horizontal lines. "The top tier is you, pastor. You're the one who is responsible to communicate the vision, the strategy, and the plan in a clear, compelling way. But who is your first and primary audience?" On the second tier, I wrote, "The leadership team." I asked everyone, "What would happen if the pastor communicated the plan to the congregation, but you weren't on board?"

"Ahhh," some of them sighed. And one spoke for the rest: "It would be a disaster!"

"Precisely. There's a big difference in the effectiveness of broadcasting a vision to everyone and cascading the communication of the vision to particular groups. Let's talk about what it means to cascade. So…the pastor's first audience is you. It's imperative for him to share his heart, clarify direction, and show each of you how you can be involved in reaching far more people for Christ." They were nodding now. "And then each of you will play key roles in communicating to the next tier of people." It took a few seconds for that to sink in, and then I asked, "Who is the next audience?"

Someone piped up, "I'm guessing it's not the congregation!" Everyone laughed.

"Exactly right," I answered. "Then who is it?"

The pastor answered, "We need to get the governing board of elders and our deacons to sign on to this. Without them…" No one needed him to complete his sentence.

I asked, "Are there important leaders in the church who don't have titles?"

Someone said, "Of course!"

The pastor jumped in, "And I'm thinking it would be good to have the top donors informed well before the rest of the congregation so they get excited about their participation."

"Now you're getting it! And for each new tier, everyone in the one above it will have a part in the communication of the vision and the strategy."

Someone jumped in, "So the number of people sharing the vision grows at each stage."

"Exactly."

One of the team members asked, "Okay, I get it, but when do we tell the congregation?"

I wrote "Congregation" on the next to last tier, and I said, "Only when you've gotten buy-in from all the tiers above them on the pyramid."

"And who are the people below the congregation?" someone asked.

"The community. When the momentum has built over time, the people in your church will be telling their friends and acquaintances about the new vision. And the local media will want to carry information about what you're doing."

The pastor sat back in his chair and reflected, "So…we need a communication strategy that gradually builds momentum, includes more people, answers more questions, and has people in each tier communicating to the one below it…and the success doesn't depend only on me to get everyone to sign on."

The pastor smiled. "Sam, what do you call this?"

"Cascading communication." By this time, we had the pyramid filled in.

This pyramid is one of the ways a church might be organized. Yours may have more or fewer layers. Look at this one:[38]

We spent the rest of the meeting talking about the who, when, where, and how of the cascading communication strategy. The broadcast of the vision to the congregation and the community doesn't happen until each tier has been addressed, encouraged, and enlisted to carry the message of change. Damage can happen if leaders communicate too much too soon to too many. Quite often, unfounded rumors short-circuit good plans, and natural resistance to change is enflamed instead of overcome. This, I believe, is one of the most common struggles organizations have when their leaders launch a fresh vision and try to implement the plans. The lack of a communication strategy creates unnecessary fears, which erodes trust and causes people to become entrenched in their positions. A workable, cascading communication plan multiplies the vision carriers, builds enthusiasm, and usually results in a much smoother process of change.

> **DAMAGE CAN HAPPEN IF LEADERS COMMUNICATE TOO MUCH TOO SOON TO TOO MANY. UNFOUNDED RUMORS CAN SHORT-CIRCUIT GOOD PLANS, AND NATURAL RESISTANCE TO CHANGE IS ENFLAMED.**

Each tier of people has specific needs for information. For this reason, the skeleton remains the same, but the *meat on the bones* will be tailored to each audience. This is a plan I often recommend to pastors and business leaders:

1. Each meeting builds on the previous meeting—the people in the second tier attend the meeting for the third tier, those in the third tier will attend the meeting for the fourth tier, and so on.

2. In each meeting, communicate why you're talking to that specific group. In other words, communicate how each group specifically can contribute to the fulfillment of the vision.

3. In the meeting, affirm the people in previous tiers (who are in the room) for their commitment to the project.

4. Always use examples and illustrations that are relevant to the tier you're addressing. For instance, the benefits you describe for the staff team will be somewhat different from the ones you'll explain to the key donors or the small group leaders or the community.

5. Communicate a clear direction, enough specifics, and the right amount of emotion so people will know this is important to you.

6. For the first two or three tiers, don't have a time for questions and answers because you probably don't have enough answers yet, and it doesn't look good for you to say, "I don't know," too many times. As you get more answers and feel more comfortable, have a time for questions and answers as you communicate down the tiers.

7. Before you end, ask, "What is the primary message you're taking from this meeting?" This accomplishes two things: first, it lets you know how much they understood your vision; and second, their verbalization reinforces their commitment to it. You may realize that you need to clarify a point or emphasize something specific for this group.

8. Even when you have time for questions and answers, don't end when this is finished. Instead, ask the question about what they're taking from the meeting, and then end on a high note with a closing statement to share your heart and your hope for the church or business.

9. It's possible to host several tiers back to back to back on a Saturday, scheduling thirty to forty-five minutes for each one with a short break between them. The talking points will remain the same, but the illustrations will change for each audience. Each group will be involved in at least two of these meetings: one when they hear the vision for the first time and the second when they hear you communicate to the next tier.

10. After this *deep seeding* of the tiers of leaders has happened, preach a series to the congregation, including four messages:

+ First weekend: communicate an overview of the vision.

+ Second and third weekend: share the plan and benefits.

+ Fourth weekend: talk about the difference the change will make in the congregation and the community. Create a buzz with T-shirts, banners, a page on the website, posts on social media, and maybe a new song about the vision.

A clear and compelling vision will have three significant effects. It will:

1. *Synergize*, bringing people together to cooperate and organizing plans for maximum impact

2. *Galvanize*, inviting strong and deep commitment

3. *Energize*, creating enthusiasm and participation

When can a leader use a cascading communication strategy? Any time there's a significant change in direction, any time it's possible to be misunderstood, and any time you anticipate resistance. In other words, more often than you may think!

The tension for most leaders is that they are platform people who are used to broadcasting their message to everyone who will listen, but when they're changing the direction of the church, they need to slow down, identify the tiers of leadership and involvement, and patiently get commitments from one before going to the next.

THE SILENT GENERATION TO GEN Z

Hundreds of thousands, perhaps millions, of pages have been written about the differences between generations. We don't need to get deep in the weeds of all the differences. Instead, I want to focus on some insights and principles that will help leaders connect with the minds and hearts of all ages of people.

Generally, as generations move from the oldest to the youngest, people gradually shift from the concrete to the abstract and emotional. Earlier in the book, we looked at the differences in how each generation views work. Here, we focus on the different ways they communicate.

+ *The Silent Generation* (born between 1925 and 1945) has this label because most of the people in this era suffered through the Great Depression and World War II by working hard without complaining. The trauma of those two great events was followed by the threats of the Cold War with the Soviet Union and anti-communist sentiment. People were afraid to speak out, so their opinions were effectively silenced. They are rapidly leaving the scene in our communities.

+ *Boomers* (born between 1946 and 1964) are typically goal-oriented and value financial rewards and prestige. They don't require very much affirming feedback.

+ Xers (born between 1965 and 1980) often react to the drive of their parents and instead pursue work-life balance. Still, they're dreamers. They make up 55 percent of startup companies.

+ *Millennials* (born after 1980) have been studied incessantly to discover what makes them different than the other generations. Many managers have tried to figure out what motivates them. Millennials see their skills as assets to hire for profit, and they're always ready to find a better job. They prefer flexible schedules, and the work environment may be more important than the pay.

+ *Generation Z* (born after 2000) thrive on technology because they've grown up with it, but over half prefer interpersonal communication. A study by Deloitte shows that the young people in this segment will be the largest and most diverse in the country in the next few years. Since they grew up in the wake of the Great Recession, experts assumed they'd be "a pragmatic, risk-averse, non-entrepreneurial group motivated by job security." But the study revealed a different picture: they "value salary less than every other generation: if given the choice of accepting a better-paying but boring job versus work that was more interesting but didn't pay as well, Gen Z was fairly evenly split over the choice.... Companies and employers will need to highlight their efforts to be good global citizens. And actions speak louder than words: Companies must demonstrate their commitment to a broader set of societal challenges such as sustainability, climate change, and hunger."[39]

I believe the passion, talents, and idealism of Gen Z has the potential to be the greatest force for good since the dramatic surge in social involvement and missions after World War II.

> **YOUNGER LEADERS CAN MISUNDERSTAND THE DRIVE AND LOYALTY OF THE OLDER GENERATION, AND OLDER LEADERS CAN MISINTERPRET THE FLEXIBILITY OF YOUNG PEOPLE AS A LACK OF COMMITMENT.**

We typically "speak the language" of the people in our generation. Younger leaders can misunderstand the drive and loyalty of the older generation, and older leaders can misinterpret the flexibility of young people as a lack of commitment. In an article for *Inc.*, the author quotes corporate trainer Bruce Mayhew:

> To manage across generations, we have to learn to be mindful of each other and treat each other as individuals. No matter what generation we are from, it's too easy to keep doing what we are doing now and acting like each generation is (or should be) motivated by the same things we are.... We always have to be mindful of our actions and stay open to listening to each other. Use everyone's ability and goals.[40]

Many of the people who have been around for a long time are quite content for your organization to keep the same culture and programs. They resist change, but their resistance effectively closes the door to people who are creative, full of energy, and bring a sense of adventure. This is a tension virtually all pastors feel. Is it possible to bridge the gap between generations? In an article in *Christianity Today* titled "The Price of Progress," Pastor Stuart Briscoe advises pastors to ask if a decision will take the church toward or away from their primary mission. Asking hard questions, he observes, will often produce difficult answers. He tells the story about an encounter shortly after he became the pastor at Elmbrook Church. He discovered that a hundred young people were meeting at the home of a couple in the church. That was great news, but then he learned they had all dropped out of church because they felt it was irrelevant. He decided to go to the house to meet them. When he asked why they felt that way, one of them spoke up, "We've gotten the message we're not welcome."

Briscoe looked around at the whole group and told him, "Well, you're absolutely welcome. Not only are you welcome, it's imperative you come at once. You need to belong to a fellowship of believers, and we need your drive and enthusiasm."

Two weeks later on a Sunday morning, they showed up…and they had come to Briscoe's straight-laced church wearing T-shirts and jeans. "One wore an American flag sewed to the seat of her pants. Others wore oversized crosses that looked as if they had been pilfered from an archbishop." The people in the congregation looked at them with a mixture of suspicion and horror.

A few days later, one of the lay leaders came to Briscoe's office. He voiced his concern. He explained that he and his wife—and many other parents of their generation in the church—had worked very hard to keep their teenagers away from bad influences like the kids who had come to church that week. He insisted that Briscoe keep them away from the young people who regularly attended the church. He finished with the demanding question, "Do you understand?"

"Of course, I understand," Briscoe replied. "The policy you're suggesting is similar to the one they have in South Africa. It's called apartheid, and it's based on prejudice and fear." Briscoe wanted to identify with the man's concern while still correcting his perspective. He continued, "I understand those emotions because I struggle with them myself. But they have absolutely no place in the community of believers. I'm committed in this church to this kind of diversity."

He was making *the* decision about the direction of the church, which would result in thousands of other decisions as a consequence. We might suspect that the layman walked out in an angry huff, but he didn't. When he realized Briscoe wouldn't budge, he offered to begin a class for parents who are struggling with their teenagers. Briscoe was shocked by the offer and readily agreed. The class proved so successful that soon it had a waiting list of people who wanted to attend. Less than a year later, the class ended with no plans for the next semester. When Briscoe asked why they were stopping, the man explained, "Because the issues have been resolved." In fact, in a dramatic and stunning reversal, students who didn't attend the church began asking adults in the church to help them understand their parents.

The decision to welcome teenagers into the life of the church was, I'm sure, one that Briscoe would identify as one of the most important in his ministry. It had a long-term impact, and its influence was both deep and wide. He concluded, "If we're going to weather a tempest, let it be because we're sailing in a mighty ocean rather than in a teapot."[41]

The Scriptures show a clear pattern of the importance of passing the mantle of leadership from one generation to the next. The patriarchs had a family lineage from Abraham to Isaac to Jacob. Moses trained and equipped Joshua to lead the people across the Jordan to the Promised Land. Elijah became the mentor for Elisha and trained him so well that Elisha asked for and received a "double portion" of spiritual power from God. We see the transfer of authority clearly in Paul's letter to Timothy. He instructed his young protégé:

> You then, my son, be strong in the grace that is in Christ Jesus. And the things you have heard me say in the presence of many witnesses entrust to reliable people who will also be qualified to teach others.
>
> (2 Timothy 2:1–2)

Paul wasn't content for only Timothy to thrive in leadership. He envisioned four generations of believers, with the implication that the transfer would continue until Jesus returns: Paul to Timothy to reliable people and to others. Paul and Timothy had to figure out how to connect with and motivate people in subsequent generations. So do we.

SILENT AND VOCAL

Like likes like. This means that leaders are usually most impressed with people who are like them: verbal and enthusiastic. They gravitate to those who are articulate and who are, at least occasionally, a bit too verbose. Preachers value preachers, visionaries appreciate visionaries, and excited people like to be with others who have passion for a cause. These leaders may assume that a quiet person isn't engaged and, in fact, is bored. I've found that this is often a misplaced assumption.

I've been in an executive team meeting when one of the people (I'll call her Janice) dives in to the leader's idea and eagerly offers ways to make it happen. Throughout the meeting, Janice is on the edge of her seat, commenting on others' ideas, affirming the leader's statements, and adding a shot of adrenaline to every part of the conversation. During all this time, another person on the team (I'll call him Bill) has been listening and jotting notes, but he hasn't volunteered a word. When the leader asks for input about a particular idea, Bill listens and nods, but he doesn't offer an opinion. As the meeting ends and the leader gives assignments, who do you think gets the most important role? Janice, of course. The leader is convinced that her verbal skills will translate into management talent.

He doesn't overlook Bill. Quite the contrary, he's very much aware that Bill has been silent, and he has come to the conclusion that Bill has been doodling or writing a note to someone instead of paying attention. A week later, when Janice has struggles putting concepts into practice because she lacks management skills, the leader is surprised, but he gives her a pass. (It has happened many times before.) But the leader has failed to tap into Bill's extraordinary abilities to plan, strategize, delegate, and manage tasks. He only gives Bill the most mundane of tasks, and he doesn't even follow up to see how well Bill has performed his role. The leader has drawn very strong conclusions based on which staff member's verbal skills are most like his—which has led to two mistakes in his leadership.

A wise leader recognizes this tension; poor leaders make assumptions. In every meeting, one or two people are more verbal than the others, but they may not be the right choice to organize a program or lead a team to accomplish a specific goal.

All of us live with the tension of knowing when to speak up and when to remain silent. (Ask your spouse and you'll find out!) We need to read the situation, read the person, read our natural tendencies, and make any necessary adjustments. The vast majority of the time, I don't need to say anything to Brenda to correct her thinking because she's already aware of it. On the other hand, she often needs to overcome her natural reluctance and speak up to challenge my thinking or plans (or lack of plans). When those of us who often speak address an audience, we need to *read the room* and tailor our points and our stories to fit the moment. In the same way, husbands, wives, parents, leaders, team members, and friends need to read the person in front of them and speak appropriately...or not at all.

We've heard the old saying, "Sticks and stones can break my bones, but words can never hurt me." That's perhaps the most inaccurate statement I've ever heard. Words have incredible power to hurt or heal.

James reminds us to be very careful about what comes out of our mouths:

> We all stumble in many ways. Anyone who is never at fault in what they say is perfect, able to keep their whole body in check.... With the tongue we praise our Lord and Father, and with it we curse human beings, who have been made in God's likeness. Out of the same mouth come praise and cursing. My brothers and sisters, this should not be. Can both fresh water and salt water flow from the same spring? My brothers and sisters, can a fig tree bear olives, or a grapevine bear figs? Neither can a salt spring produce fresh water.
>
> (James 3:2, 9–12)

For people who are verbal like me, it's tempting to fill any silence with a lot of words. I'm afraid that too many times, I've prevented people from sharing gold because I was too quick to jump in and fill the air with copper. If I'd waited two more seconds, I'd have heard something wise and wonderful, but I was impatient.

In his letter to the Thessalonians, Paul gives us a clear framework for our communication:

And we urge you, brothers and sisters, warn those who are idle and disruptive, encourage the disheartened, help the weak, be patient with everyone. (1 Thessalonians 5:14)

Read the person, read the emotions, and read the pressure the person is under, and then speak appropriately.

> **SOMETIMES, WE NEED THE COURAGE TO SPEAK UP, AND SOMETIMES, WE NEED THE WISDOM TO HOLD OUR TONGUES. WE ALWAYS NEED THE DISCERNMENT TO KNOW THE DIFFERENCE.**

Sometimes, we need the courage to speak up, and sometimes, we need the wisdom to hold our tongues, and we always need the discernment to know the difference. We live in a noisy world, and it seems everybody is always plugged in to a phone or listening to music or podcasts or something else. Don't get me wrong: I'm not saying these things are evil or wrong, but I am suggesting that we need at least some time every day for silence. Our minds can't unclutter when we're continually filling them with sounds.

BLUNT AND KIND

In Paul's letter to the Christians in Ephesus, he spends the first three chapters describing the foundation of faith. Then in the last three chapters, he explains what genuine faith looks like in real life—or rather, I should say, what it *can* look like. A short but powerful statement about our relationships is that God wants us to be *"speaking the truth in love"* (Ephesians 4:15). That, as I'm sure you're aware, is easier said than done.

We tend to lean in one direction or the other. Some of us are committed to tell the truth no matter how it sounds to the listeners. We claim that's what Jesus did in His conversations with the Pharisees, and we feel completely justified in blasting away. Our message comes across as harsh and condemning, especially to sensitive people. Why do we bludgeon people with truth? Because it's effective: most people are so intimidated that they let us have our way.

But others of us are on the other end of the stick. Maybe we've been hurt by harsh words in the past, or maybe it's just our temperament to be gentle, but whatever the cause, we lean hard toward kindness... sometimes at the expense of truth. We rationalize that we don't want to hurt anyone's feelings, they won't respond well, they can't help it, or their offensive behavior really isn't all that bad. When the chips are down and a frank conversation is needed, we leave the table.

AVOIDING THE TENSION BETWEEN BOLDNESS AND KINDNESS PUSHES US TO BECOME EITHER SELF-JUSTIFYING LIONS OR HARMLESS LAMBS.

"Truth in love." Boldness *and* kindness. Both—not one or the other. Avoiding the tension pushes us to one of the two ends, and we become either self-justifying lions or harmless lambs, and we feel perfectly fine about it! To live in the tension, we need to know ourselves and know our audience, even if it's only one person. Those who tend to speak truth without love need to sit back, calm down, recognize that we're using truth to manipulate and get our way, and engage at a far lower intensity—asking questions that show we value the person, not questions that are thinly disguised hammers. And those of us who don't want to

hurt a fly by saying something that might be corrective need to realize our hesitancy is really cowardice. We're protecting ourselves instead of valuing the integrity of the relationship.

One of the most important leadership principles I've learned is that people are different. (Yes, I know you're thinking this fact is abundantly obvious!) When we relate to people on our teams or in our families, it's not always the best approach to *"treat them the way we want to be treated."* I'm sure that sounds heretical, but let me explain. We need to know our audience—the person sitting across from us. All some people need is the slightest hint that they need to change their attitude or behavior, and that's enough to effect real change. But other people need a more direct approach: they don't get it if we're too circumspect and evasive. They need us to look them in the eye, describe their error, and clearly describe what the change looks like. The problem, of course, is that the sensitive people are exceptionally responsive to the second method, the bold one, but they often respond out of fear and shame. And the others—we'll call them less sensitive people—completely miss the point if we're not bold enough. I believe many of the problems we have in relationships are the result of not understanding our audience. We're too harsh with the sensitive and too mild with those who need us to be frank.

Let me identify one more tension point related to boldness and kindness. Some of us are radically different in one arena than another. We may be tigers online, spouting extreme views on anything that inflames our passions, but a harmless lamb in person. Or we may be fearless on the platform, but unwilling to say hard things in person or to our teams. Integrity is being the same person everywhere and in every relationship.

Know your tendency to be on one end or the other, and know the person you're talking to. With the wisdom we gain from this dual perception, we'll tailor our communication to fit the moment.

PERSONAL AND DIGITAL

How many times have you sent an email or text that wasn't received in exactly the way you intended? I've done that. And how many times have you sent a sensitive email to the wrong person? Yeah, me too. I love modern technology and the incredible opportunities to connect with people—those in the next room and those on the other side of the world. But we need to understand both the power of digital communication and its limitations.

Personal connections (face-to-face, video conferencing, and phone) are necessary in a number of instances, including when:

+ Emotion must be communicated accurately

+ The relationship is vulnerable

+ You're using nuance, like humor, that can easily be misinterpreted

+ *All caps* don't capture the tone you want to express

+ You can't take the risk of being misunderstood

One leader suggests always moving one step toward being more personable: if you'd send a quick text, send an email; if you'd email, make a call; if you'd make a phone call, do a video call; if you'd make a video call, make an appointment to have coffee or lunch with the person. And any time you send a text or email, read it twice and double check the name on the addressee line! It takes a few seconds longer, but if you don't, I guarantee there will be times when you wish you had.

ANY TIME YOU SEND A TEXT OR EMAIL, READ IT TWICE AND DOUBLE CHECK THE NAME ON THE ADDRESSEE LINE! IF YOU DON'T, I GUARANTEE THERE WILL BE TIMES WHEN YOU WISH YOU HAD.

Soft skills of personal communication are hard to measure, but are powerful in shaping the culture of a relationship or an organization. Today, we can collaborate on projects and plan events very efficiently using technology, but we need to remember the benefits of personal connections. Remote workplaces are convenient and efficient, but they seldom produce shared values and a sense of community. When we're physically together, we can pick up on nonverbal messages and body language that's missing in texts, email, and even phone conversations. Face-to-face contacts give both parties greater opportunities to clarify anything that has been misunderstood. In an article about the upside of closer connections, Megan Baker and Jelena Milutinovic comment:

> When addressing sensitive issues, put down the phone, move away from the keyboard, and make the effort to engage in-person—it will be crucial to a successful outcome. Whether you are providing specific feedback to a staff member or addressing an issue with a colleague, much can be misinterpreted or lost when communicating via technology. Focus on your desired outcome and prepare by considering the mindset and possible reactions of the one you will be communicating with. This can help to turn a challenging conversation into a trust-building interaction.[42]

Many churches have made great strides in the past few years to catch up with their business counterparts in using technology to connect with constituents. They post sermons on their websites and provide a wide range of important information for people who are curious about the church as well as those who are regular attendees. In addition, quite a few pastors have a strong presence on social media. The landscape is always changing, however, so it's important for church leaders to regularly ask three questions:

1. What is the quality of our current technology?

2. What aspects of our technology need improvement?

3. What new technology would enhance our outreach?

Technology has made it easy for people to *go to church* without actually showing up. They can watch and listen...and not just to their own pastor, but leading pastors across the country and the world. That's not good or bad; it's just a fact. We need to be sure, though, that we don't get the technological wagon in front of the horse of mission.

In an article titled "Grow Your Church by Embracing Technology," author Daniel Threlfall gives this advice:

> **Relate technology to the church mission.** Without a clear church mission, any church is bound to flounder in all areas, not just technology. A strong church mission serves as a tether to secure churches to a biblical mooring. This is not the place for a discussion of church mission, but it may serve you well to give serious thought to developing a church mission, and then relating church technology to its proper place within the mission of the church. Remember, the mission should come first, followed by integration of technology.[43]

Communication is the lifeblood of a leader. We live in multiple tensions, but with some insights to sharpen our focus and eliminate distractions, we'll share a clearer vision, move more hearts, and accomplish more for God's kingdom. Isn't that why we're doing this anyway?

THINK ABOUT IT:

1. How would you identify the tiers in your church or business?

2. What are the benefits of cascading your communication of a significant change in the direction of your business or church?

3. What are your biggest challenges in communicating to multiple generations? How are you meeting (or going to meet) those challenges?

4. Who are the people on your team who are most like you? Do you find yourself leaning toward them to value their opinions and talents more than others? Be honest, and explain your answer.

5. Where are you on the continuum of bluntness and kindness? (Hint: you almost certainly don't have perfect balance!)

6. When is face-to-face (or at least voice-to-voice) communication necessary?

APPLY IT:

♦ As you read this chapter, what tensions described here reminded you of your experiences?

♦ How did you respond at the time?

♦ How do you want to respond next time?

♦ Who do you know who is experiencing a similar tension today?

♦ How can you help this person embrace the tension, resolve the tension, or use the tension to stimulate an innovative solution?

9

MANAGING TENSION
(BEFORE IT MANAGES YOU!)

Maturity is achieved when a
person accepts life as full of tension.
—Joshua L. Liebman

It is inherent in the role of leadership to create tension. By definition, leaders take people to places that are unfamiliar, often uncomfortable, and even threatening. We might even say that the first job of a great leader is to increase the level of stress. Some might even call it chaos. If we don't understand this basic fact, we'll be caught off guard when we sense tension on our teams, we'll back down instead of pushing ahead, and we'll become paralyzed by the fear of disapproval.

When leaders are afraid of tension, they send a loud and clear signal that they're abdicating their responsibility to lead. Tension is inescapable: how we handle it either increases our leadership equity or drains it dry. Trying to avoid sticky conversations only leads to more tension and lower credibility.

Years ago when I was leading an organization, a couple of people on our executive team weren't getting along...to put it mildly. They looked for ways to undermine each other, smiling as they voiced snarky comments, and obviously delighting if the other struggled with any assignment. For months, I hoped they would work it out; occasionally, I talked to them privately to offer friendly advice about working together more effectively, such as believing the best in each other, and similar well-worn relational ideas. But nothing changed. In fact, their mutual animosity gradually got worse. Finally, I'd had enough.

The team came to my office for our weekly meeting. I had sent them the agenda a few days earlier so they could be prepared, but as we started, I told them, "You can put your agendas away. We're going to talk about what's going on with our team." Every eye suddenly shot up and focused on me. I had their attention and everyone knew what the topic would be. I continued, "I'm going to make observations about what's been happening with our team, and I'm going to ask each of you to share your observations. You may agree with my perceptions, you may disagree, or you may agree, but have a different angle on things. Please don't feel that you have to see things the way I see them. Just be honest. That's all I ask."

At that moment, I'm not sure anybody in the room was still breathing. Without any further introduction, I began. I'll call the two combatants Phil and Javier. I pointed to one of the two men and then the other, but I spoke to the whole team: "Phil and Javier have been at odds for a long time. I hoped they could work out the problems between them, but they haven't. Their seething resentment has directly affected each of them, and it has indirectly affected all of us. Their anger and passive-aggressive behavior show up in their interactions with each other, and it puts all of us on edge. Because of this, we're less effective than we could be. We're more guarded than we could be, and we can't talk at the level of honesty and vulnerability that we need in order to be the best leaders we can be. I've spent far too much of my time and energy trying to manage their conflict. Today, it has to stop. That's my read of the situation. What's yours? I'll let Phil and Javier speak last, but I want to hear from the rest of you first."

There were six of us in the room, so I was asking three people to speak up. But there was silence for a long, awkward minute. Finally, one of them said, "Well, I don't want to add to the problem, and I'm sure Javier and Phil mean well, but yes, I've seen a little bit of tension between them."

The second one spoke up, "Yes, there's been some disagreement between them, but I'm sure they've misunderstood each other. They both have good hearts. We all have bad days, and maybe we've seen them on their bad days."

The third was bold and honest. He began, "I've seen it for a long time." Then he looked at me and said, "And frankly, I wondered if you even saw it. I'm glad we're finally talking about it, and I hope they can resolve their differences so we can function as a team."

I asked Phil and Javier if they wanted to say anything. They looked at each other and then shook their heads. I turned to the two of them and announced, "The four of us are going to leave the room. You two are staying. Next week, you can report to us how you've resolved your dispute. If not, we're going to make some major changes. We simply cannot go on this way any longer." And with that, I stood up. The other three quickly grabbed their files and papers, and the four of us walked out.

My goal wasn't to resolve the tension in this executive team meeting. In fact, I injected more tension by putting our agenda aside and calling out the two men. Then, I created an even higher level of tension when I asked the other three to articulate their observations. And I let the two men marinate in tension juices for a week before they would give us a report on how they resolved their resentment...or their report on how they failed to resolve it.

A week later, I sent the agenda for the meeting to the five people. The first item said simply: outcome. Everyone knew what the word referred to. As people walked in, they tried to avoid eye contact because they didn't know what to expect. When everyone was seated, I turned to Phil and Javier and said, "The first item on the agenda is the outcome of your attempt at resolution. Tell us what happened."

Phil began. He said he and Javier had a very productive series of conversations during the week, beginning in the room right after the other four of us left the previous week. They realized they agreed on some important issues, and they disagreed on others. They concluded that their relationship was more important than their opposing points of view, and they apologized to each other for the harm they'd caused. Javier sat nodding through Phil's explanation, and then he told us, "That's right. We apologized to each other, and we plan to talk regularly to set a new tone in our relationship. We also want to apologize to all of you."

The rest of us nodded in approval, and I said, "Very good. Let's move on to the second item on our agenda." I was so proud of my self-control at that moment. Everything in me wanted to rehash everything that had happened between Phil and Javier over the past year, explaining in detail how each of them had acted and the ways they had adversely affected our team. And I wanted them to express the pain they felt in elaborate terms. To be honest, I wanted to talk about how crucial this was to our team, but only because the severity of the problem and the power of the resolution would affirm my leadership. Yes, I wanted all that, but instead, I just affirmed their mutual resolution and moved on. This was a pivotal moment for Phil and Javier, an important step for our team, and a good lesson for me in how to lead.

INTENTIONAL TENSION

We create tension in many different ways, and some of them are quite intentional. For our executive team, I had avoided shining a spotlight on *the elephant in the room* for a long, long time, but when I did, no one could hide. The team finally knew I saw what they saw, and I wasn't afraid to call it out. They also saw that my steps of resolution didn't make me the center of attention. I asked for everyone to be honest about what they'd seen in the ongoing dispute, and I asked the two of them to work things out. This process certainly raised the level of tension on our team, but it was absolutely necessary. Before that day when I spoke into the conflict, the team may have wondered if I valued our relationships, but after that day, they didn't doubt it any longer.

I believe people on teams intuitively ask a number of questions about the leader when conflict isn't addressed:

+ Does he see what I see?

+ If he doesn't see it, how can he be so blind?

+ Will he ever see it?

+ If he sees it and hasn't done anything about it, can I trust him?

> **FIND THE COURAGE TO WADE INTO TENSION ON YOUR TEAM OR IN YOUR FAMILY. INVITE DISCUSSION, AFFIRM OBSERVATIONS, AND ASK PEOPLE TO PARTICIPATE IN THE RESOLUTION.**

The moral to the story is to find the courage to wade into tension on your team or in your family. Your first impulse may be to run and hide, or to clamp down and control, but instead, invite discussion, affirm observations, and ask people to participate in the resolution. There are, I believe, two kinds of interpersonal tension: destructive and productive. We need insight to see which is which.

We're all familiar with the proverb, *"As iron sharpens iron, so one person sharpens another"* (Proverbs 27:17). When iron sharpens iron, sparks fly! Don't be afraid of that. Disagreement can be very healthy because it forces people to think more clearly and plan more effectively. But at the point when pressure becomes unbearable, iron crushes. When we see this happening, it's time to step in, speak the truth, and invite people to enter a process of self-discovery and resolution.

In an article for *Entrepreneur*, Dr. David G. Javitch lists "7 Steps to Defuse Workplace Tension." He recommends that we step back and see the big picture in our workplace interpersonal stresses:

> I suggest that conflict does not need to be characterized as just negative. In fact, it can be neutral or even positive. Conflict can simply be defined as tension. Tension can be good, bad or neutral. Just because two people disagree doesn't mean their disagreement is negative or poisonous; it can simply be a difference of opinion. However, left unaddressed and allowed to fester or grow, that neutral tension can become negative and possibly harmful. Then everyone, including the organization, suffers. Whatever definition is used, we can agree that most people don't like conflict. Indeed, they go out of their way to avoid it. In many cases, people view conflict in terms of arguments, anger, hurt feelings or being yelled at. And no one likes those situations. As a result, when conflict arises, most people will steer clear of it or pretend it doesn't exist. Nonetheless, it is real, and it may become problematic.[44]

Two of the steps Javitch recommends are to help both parties find common ground and encourage compromise. Both people have a stake in the outcome, and it's important for the leader to build a bridge between them...or at least offer a bridge and see if they'll walk onto it. Then, each one can give a little to gain a lot—sometimes including continued employment! Painful feelings don't change overnight, but each person can make a commitment to speak with civility and act with integrity.

Over time, resentment can turn into respect. They don't have to become best friends, but for a team to operate, a baseline of mutual respect is essential.

Sometimes, resolving an existing tension opens the door to the tension of new possibilities. After Phil and Javier had their talk and came back to our team with renewed commitment to cooperation, all of us felt more at ease, and their agreement gave them the freedom to question each other without the strong undercurrents of suspicion and resentment. Now, they seemed to actually enjoy their arguments, much to the surprise of the rest of us. They also lived with the new realization that I was no longer going to act like I didn't see what was going on. Phil and Javier—and the other three on the team—became aware that I was going to address any tension that was harmful to our team. I had put them all on notice.

We aren't going to have a tension-free life until we're in the presence of Jesus. When we resolve a tension, we need to be aware that we're setting the stage for a new, higher, and hopefully more productive form. In this way, we go from tension to tension, always learning, always growing, and always teaching others how to handle it.

We also intentionally create tension by asking what's working and why it's working. Most organizations focus their attention on what's not working, and they spend inordinate amounts of time and effort to fix it. I've found that it's more productive (and encouraging) to devote more resources to make successes even better. Questioning failure creates tension that often demoralizes. Questioning success creates tension, but it affirms and inspires.

QUESTIONING FAILURE CREATES TENSION THAT OFTEN DEMORALIZES. QUESTIONING SUCCESS CREATES TENSION, BUT IT AFFIRMS AND INSPIRES.

BLESSED AMBIGUITY

Most of us avoid tension, and if we have to wade into it, we want it to be over as quickly as possible. In conflict, this often pushes us to take sides with one person over the other. A power play may seem to be a good solution, but it invariably increases the level of tension and results in even more intense conflict later. The person we supported appreciates us, but the other one often feels more than misunderstood—he feels betrayed.

I've found it's a good idea to avoid taking sides except in cases of truth and integrity. In the vast majority of situations, disputes are about opinions, preferences, and processes. I ask both people to come to see me, and I ask each one to tell me what's going on...and I listen. Instead of jumping to a conclusion and ending the discussion, I say, "Okay, that's helpful. Tell me more about it."

When I interject a comment, I make sure it's positive. I may say, "I see some areas of disagreement, but I see that you're both trying to achieve the same goal. Different ideas aren't a threat to any of us. In fact, we'll be wiser and stronger by listening to each other."

Quite often, the two people talk for a long time, and since they're talking in front of their supervisor or team leader, they eventually look for a mutually satisfactory solution to resolve the tension. However, in a few cases, this tension-resolution strategy causes people to harden their positions. They become demanding and defensive, which tells me more than they want me to know about them. When this happens, I address the problem beneath the problem, and again, this process gives me valuable insights into the hearts, minds, and motives of the people involved.

STAY ENGAGED IN THE UNDERSTANDING PHASE OF A CONVERSATION LONG ENOUGH SO THAT YOU CAN ARTICULATE THE OTHER PERSON'S POINT OF VIEW AS WELL AS HE CAN.

One of the principles I've found to be helpful is to stay engaged in the understanding phase of a conversation long enough so that I can articulate the other person's point of view as well (or almost as well) as he can. The first task of a counselor is for the person to feel understood, and one of the most important tasks of a leader is for team members (and anyone else) to feel that we understand them. It takes time, but we're far more likely to win a friend and build trust if we ask a few more questions, listen a little longer, and then say, "This is what I hear you saying." After we've defined the other person's position, she can say, "Yes, that's exactly what I'm saying," or she can explain, "No, you don't quite get it. Let me try again." Either way, we're communicating the more important message that we value the person more than winning the dispute.

CHOOSING TENSIONS

We can identify three kinds of tension:

1. the kind that needs to be *resolved,* like the conflict between Phil and Javier

2. the kind that can be *overlooked*

3. the kind that is *good, healthy, and productive* because it pushes us to be our best

If we can identify which of these categories a particular tension falls into, we'll have a good head start on how to respond. We've already analyzed at least one kind that needs resolution, but we can't go around jumping into every tension we see every day. We need to do a kind of *tension triage,* devoting our attention to a few and ignoring the others (at least for the moment). We don't deny those exist, and we don't tell others they don't matter, but we don't spend our time trying to put out every brushfire on our team, in our organization, or at home.

A TEAM MEMBER'S INCOMPETENCE CREATES TENSION FOR THE LEADER AND EVERYONE ON THE TEAM.

A team member's incompetence creates tension for the leader and everyone on the team. Everyone has to spend time thinking about how to respond to the person who's usually late, unprepared, or says things that don't apply to the situation. This is like a driver whose car has stalled on the highway, leaving a mile-long back-up of frustrated drivers behind him. They can't help thinking about the mess someone else has made! Instinctively, responsible people on the team try to fill in the gaps, so the irresponsible person can create a cascade of new decisions by the leader and other people on the team. I applaud these people for their willingness to put the team's goals above their personal convenience, but this is another point when I need to step in to address the tension in the room.

I can't resolve every tension; in fact, I can't even address all of them. I envision myself on the end of a dozen ropes. Each one has someone who is trying to pull me in a direction. I can't play tug-of-war with all of them, so I have to choose. I may pick up only one rope in a day, or I may pick up two or three. If I don't pick up a rope, there's no tug, no tension. I have to be sure, though, that I can handle the tugs. The ropes are always there, but my choices can vary widely based on my time, my capacity, and the existing situations. When I let a rope lay on the floor, I'm not saying it doesn't exist. I'm only saying that today isn't the day for me to pick it up and feel the tension. I don't feel guilty for making these decisions. I recognize my limitations, and I also recognize that if I tried to hold them all, I wouldn't be able to respond well to any of them. They'll still be there tomorrow, and tomorrow may be the right day for me to pick one up that I walked past today.

As we've seen, many of the tensions we face are healthy. We experience them because we're pushing for more, helping people take bold steps, and reaching for greater goals. These only become toxic if we push too hard, if we don't listen to people's concerns, or if we feel so uncomfortable with the tension that we back away from the opportunities.

THE GOOD SIDE OF FAILURE

The true measure of leaders isn't their list of glowing successes, but how they respond to delays, opposition, and failures. If our egos are so fragile that we fall apart when we hit a wall, we'll scale back our vision so failure isn't a threat, we'll fail to recruit the best people because only mediocre talents will be satisfied with small challenges, and we'll lose the respect of people who follow us.

A positive response to failure begins with rigorous self-analysis. We ask ourselves and we ask a trusted mentor, "What did I do well, and what needs improvement?" The answers provide rungs on the ladder of personal progress.

Failure can shatter our confidence and erode our enthusiasm, but growing leaders develop tenacity, a strong commitment to see opportunities in every situation. This strength of character is incredibly attractive and allows them to engage competent people who can thrive in the leader's environment.

Defeat, then, isn't the end of the world; in fact, it can be the beginning of something great. The best leaders learn from difficulties and are energized by failures. They redirect their tension away from self-pity or blaming others and toward concrete steps forward. They know they aren't helpless. No matter how high the mountain, they still have the will to climb.

Eyes that see are common, but eyes that perceive are rare. We may not have been born with an unwavering spirit, but we can develop this necessary quality. Being around leaders who exhibit consistent optimism coupled with raw honesty can transform us and give us borrowed courage. Our leadership quotient is based on our perception of our ability to find resources and enlist people to tackle the challenges in front of us. Tension, then, is in the eye of the beholder. A situation that causes one person to wilt enflames another person's passion and commitment.

TENSION IS IN THE EYE OF THE BEHOLDER. A SITUATION THAT CAUSES ONE PERSON TO WILT ENFLAMES ANOTHER PERSON'S PASSION AND COMMITMENT.

People around us—those on our teams, in our families, and in our wider circles of connections—are watching to see how we handle success and failure. If we share the credit, we build strong relationships, and if we refuse to blame others for defeats, we show them that they can trust us. Every situation, positive or negative, glorious or horrible, can have redemptive value if others see us respond with calm confidence that even difficulties will teach us some of life's most valuable lessons.

Who are our heroes? They aren't the people who have enjoyed unbroken success. They're the ones who have overcome adversity. The stories we tell, the books we read, the histories we learn, and the movies that inspire us are about people who faced long odds and clawed their way through seemingly insurmountable obstacles to achieve noble goals.

Our chief aim, then, isn't to avoid tension at all costs, but to use tension to affirm relationships, inspire courage, and build character—in ourselves and in the people we lead.

But let me offer this word of warning: don't focus too much on the tension. In other words, don't let worries about tension consume you. You'll be a more effective leader—and you'll last for much longer in the role—if you know what you love to do and you live at the crossroads of passion and talent. Yes, you'll have to wade into the mud of awkward and difficult relationships from time to time, but energize yourself with the activities at which you excel, and delegate many of the other things to talented, passionate, competent people.

Leadership is all about failure—actually, it's all about responding to failure with optimism and honesty. When you fail, get up and keep going. When others fail, turn it into a learning experience. Like great movies, turn tragedy into triumph.

Your positive response to adversity is the path to greatness.

CREATE THE CULTURE

A business leader told a friend, "I've had terrible years in the company but with terrific relationships on our team, and I've had fantastic years in business with a lot of tension on our team. I'll take the positive team culture every time."

A positive, healthy organizational culture isn't a luxury; it's a necessity, and it affects everything from office communications to employee satisfaction to the public branding. A *Forbes* article reports the research by Deloitte that 94 percent of executives and 88 percent of employees believe a strong corporate culture is essential to business success. "Deloitte's survey also found that there is a strong correlation between employees who claim to feel happy and valued at work and those who say their company has a strong culture."[45] Meaning and values are important aspects of a healthy culture. The author of the article, Alan Kohll, explains:

> Meaning and purpose are more important in the workplace now than ever. A majority of employees crave meaning and purpose in their work. Without it, job satisfaction takes a major hit. And a company certainly can't build a culture without any meaning behind its work. Create a mission statement and core values and communicate these to employees. Give employees specific examples of how their roles positively impact the company and its clients.[46]

I've written extensively about the importance of corporate and church culture and how to create one that inspires employees.[47] It's a mistake, though, to assume you can radically reorient culture with a talk or a memo or a single program. Changing culture is like a battleship changing directions: it has to be done slowly and deliberately. And don't assume a healthy culture has little or no tension. Positive environments welcome tension and use it to stimulate conversation, planning, and effectiveness.

DON'T LET TENSION RISE FROM A LACK OF CLEAR PURPOSE, AN UNWORKABLE STRATEGY, AND POOR DELEGATION. THIS IS SHOOTING YOURSELF IN THE FOOT!

Take stock of the kinds of tension you normally experience—at home, at work, in your health, and so on—and analyze your common responses to them. Don't let tension rise from a lack of clear purpose, an unworkable strategy, and poor delegation. This is shooting yourself in the foot! Great leaders aren't afraid of tension, but they don't create unnecessary tension either. They push for greater goals, and they accept the reality of the tension a big vision produces.

Every moment of every day, we're shaping the culture around us. Tension isn't the enemy. When we use it wisely to stretch people to be and do their best, it's one of our best friends. The people around us are watching to see how we handle the stresses of life and leadership. If they see us managing tension effectively, they'll follow our example, and we'll all become wiser, stronger, and better leaders.

THINK ABOUT IT:

1. What are some ways good leaders create tension? What are some positive results?

2. What are some different ways, productive and destructive, that leaders respond to interpersonal tension on a team? Which of these have you experienced? What were the results?

3. What are some consequences of a leader who avoids addressing obvious conflict on the team?

4. What are the *ropes* in front of you today? Which ones are you picking up? Why are you choosing those? What would happen if you were more selective in picking up ropes?

5. How would you describe *the good side of failure*? Is this your perspective? Explain your answer.

6. Describe the culture of your team. What can you do to make it healthier and more productive?

APPLY IT:

+ As you read this chapter, what tensions described here reminded you of your experiences?

+ How did you respond at the time?

+ How do you want to respond next time?

+ Who do you know who is experiencing a similar tension today?

+ How can you help this person embrace the tension, resolve the tension, or use the tension to stimulate an innovative solution?

10

NEW EXPECTATIONS, DIFFERENT RESULTS

Since God intends to make you like Jesus, he will take you
through the same experiences Jesus went through.
That includes loneliness, temptation, stress, criticism, rejection,
and many other problems.
—Rick Warren[48]

Any kind of significant change creates tension in an organization.
Steps of progress require people to take on more responsibility, adjust

and improve their communication with others, and make hundreds of other modifications along the way. The decline of an organization also requires adjustments because contraction causes people to wonder if their leader is competent, if their jobs will last, if they'll get paid, and how it looks to have empty seats in a church or empty offices in a business. When organizations grow, people may take too much credit and not share it, and when they plateau and fail, they look for someone else to blame.

Tension can strengthen or destroy—it's our choice. I believe that all disruption is an opportunity for innovation. That is, every challenge, whether the organization is moving forward or backward, calls the leaders to be creative in finding solutions. Good leaders intuitively ask, "How can we think about this in a fresh way?" and "How can we leverage the tension to our benefit?" The leadership principle is simple and profound: *don't ever waste a crisis!*

TURNOVER AND MORALE

I was asked to consult with a company that had a very high rate of staff turnover in the previous year. In only twelve months, a third of their employees had left, most of them with undisguised disgust and resentment. The morale of those who were left was dismal, and if it could go any lower, it was already on the way there. Their exits had a ripple effect in the community. The family members and friends of those who had left (and of many who had stayed) developed a very negative view of the company, so they stopped coming to buy. Obviously, a poor reputation in the community put even more pressure on the CEO and his team.

In my first meeting with the CEO and the team, I witnessed "a circular firing squad"—everyone was blaming everyone else. I didn't keep score, but it seemed that each member of the team got off at least one shot. They questioned each other's decisions and integrity. They freely used condemning language. Their eyes glared and their voices were loud and harsh. It was apparent to me that this wasn't the first time they'd expressed these convictions! After several people talked about the noxious culture of doubt and fear among the employees, and the fact that so many had left, the CEO tried to look on the bright side: "Well, at least we're saving money on salaries." I glanced around the room to see the expressions on everyone's faces and thought, *If looks could kill…*

When a lot of their emotional energy was spent, the CEO turned to me. Without saying a word, he motioned that it was time for me to step in and work some magic. But there was a problem: I didn't have any magic. I only had one question to ask the leadership team: "You've lost a third of your employees in the past year. Tell me, what *isn't* getting done right now?"

THE COMPANY HAD LOST ONE-THIRD OF THEIR EMPLOYEES, YET SOMEHOW, EVERYTHING WAS STILL GETTING DONE.

I could see them trying to process my question. Some were carefully imagining their spreadsheets, and others were sensing the circumstances in the company. After a long silence, one person said, "Actually, I can't think of anything. Nothing important anyway."

Almost everyone nodded or said something like, "Yes, that's right." Then someone commented, "Well, I don't think anyone is staying on top of our vendors."

Another person answered, "James used to do that, but Phyllis in our department has picked up that role."

Several more people mentioned tasks of people who had left, but in every case, someone else, sometimes in a different department, had picked up the slack. After a few more minutes, I jumped back in: "Let me ask again: A third of your employees have left, and you haven't replaced them. What isn't getting done?"

A person who had been quiet during most of the meeting spoke up: "It appears the answer is nothing."

I asked, "So, how did you decide to take on the responsibilities of those who are no longer with the company?"

A few people shrugged their shoulders, and some had faint smiles. Then one of them said, "Well, I knew it had to be done, so I did it. I don't guess it's any more complicated than that."

I turned to the others. "How about the rest of you?"

The others on the team had different reasons for shouldering the load of those who were gone. Some had been asked to expand their responsibilities, and some had complained long enough that the CEO had assigned a task to someone. The point they all saw was that in some way, everything important was still getting done.

I told them, "Let me be redundant. Is there anything lying on the floor that hasn't been picked up by one of you? Is there an ongoing task that someone needs to own?"

They all shook their heads, but by now, with a new sense of pride that they had stepped into the breech with courage and talent to keep the company going. I asked, "Are you working a little harder than you were a year ago before the exodus began?"

All of them nodded, and one said, "Yes, sometimes more than a little."

"I applaud you," I told them. "You've handled a stressful situation remarkably well. Thank you for meeting with me today."

At that, the meeting was over. I shook their hands as they left. Their demeanor was completely different as they walked out. They patted each other on the back, made plans to go together to lunch, and started talking about ways they could work together.

I had scheduled a follow-up meeting with the CEO and the senior vice president, and we walked into the CEO's office. When we sat down, I told them, "You have a fantastic opportunity to reorganize your systems and structure. The shifts are already happening even without your input, and now, you can put your stamp on the company in a way that will have a positive impact for years."

They looked surprised. Hadn't they been presiding over an unmitigated disaster? Hadn't they called me to dig them out of a deep hole? They couldn't imagine that I saw something positive and hopeful in their dire situation, but they didn't say a word. I read their expressions and explained, "I understand. A lot of feelings have been hurt, and people have been discouraged. They've been working harder than before, but with little hope for a better future. We need to come out of this meeting with a plan to give them hope. I think it would be a great idea for you to announce that you appreciate their hard work so much that each employee will receive a bonus by Friday afternoon." I could tell they were stunned by my suggestion, but I continued, "It doesn't have to break the bank. It can be $500 each, but that's a minimal cost compared to the savings of the salaries of a third of your employees. Write a letter to thank people for working so hard in such difficult circumstances. It'll be a wonderful statement to them, and it will set a course toward a more positive future. You can't really put a price on the value of affirmation. When people feel appreciated, their loyalty quotient rises dramatically. They need this. You need this. Your company needs this."

> **YOU CAN'T REALLY PUT A PRICE ON THE VALUE OF AFFIRMATION. WHEN PEOPLE FEEL APPRECIATED, THEIR LOYALTY QUOTIENT RISES DRAMATICALLY.**

The CEO immediately called someone in his accounting department and gave instructions to process checks for every employee. When he hung up the phone, I said, "Now, let's talk about what your company might look like." For the next couple of hours, we used a whiteboard to reorganize the company. From HR to sales, every department was on the examining table. We charted new positions, new reporting systems, new goals, and new incentives for excellent work.

By the end of the day, the CEO had a comprehensive plan. There were, of course, many details to be worked out, but he and the Senior

VP felt confident the changes would be very productive. The next day, he called his team to another meeting, and he explained the new vision and plan to them. They asked a lot of questions, and he asked for their input in finding answers. The mood of the room was diametrically opposite of what I'd seen just the day before. Instead of blaming each other, they looked for ways to collaborate. Instead of feeling resentful, they were excited to move ahead. Instead of feeling discouraged, they had renewed passion.

At the end of the meeting, the CEO announced that each person would be getting a significant raise. "You've earned it," he told them. "You have no idea how much I appreciate all you've done for the company...and for me." He continued, "We're going to have a six-month freeze on hiring so we can see how the new systems and structures are working—what slots we need to fill, and which ones aren't needed."

They were surprised by this announcement. The day before, when they'd walked into the first meeting with me, they'd assumed I'd fix the problem by finding a way to hire a lot of people to fill the roles of the people who had left. We hadn't done that. Instead, the CEO, the Senior VP, and I reorganized the company, relaunched the vision, and began to recreate the culture.

Six months later, I met with the company's leaders again. The mood was very upbeat as they walked into the room and sat down. I asked them to tell me about what had happened since I was with them before, and they told me a lot of stories about challenges they had faced and the progress they had made. Before the reorganization—and the injection of hope—the tension they experienced had crushed them because they hadn't interpreted their company's problems as a chance to innovate, but in the past six months, their perspective had been totally changed. Now, the tension of all the changes brought out the best in them.

After hearing their stories, I asked, "Six months ago, I asked you a question about what wasn't getting done. This time, I want to ask a different question. What opportunities have you identified that you could pursue if you had more team members? Remember: we're not staff driven; we're opportunity driven."

As they thought about my question, I drew a series of steps on the board with the words *impact, ideas, implementation,* and *impact.* I explained, "You're having an impact now, and your success is opening doors of opportunity. As you notice them, you have ideas which gradually become plans. As you implement the plans and see success, you have greater impact, which then opens the next doors, and the process continues.

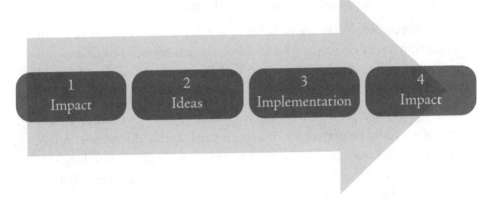

I explained each phase of progress:

+ In the first phase of impact, the leader and the team clarify the vision.

+ In the ideas phase, the team generates a lot of suggestions and recommendations to consider.

+ In the implementation phase, they curate the ideas and create a workable plan that addresses the issues of when, where, who, how, and how much. And they act on the plan to accomplish the objectives.

+ In the second impact phase, the leader and the team debrief the implementation, focusing primarily on what went right instead of what went wrong. They compare the actual outcome with the results they envisioned in the first phase.

I gave the team a couple of examples of how this simple process works. For instance, if an organization is planning another annual event simply because they do it every year, they can go through these steps. They might discover a much better way to deliver a greater impact.

At that point, the team identified two opportunities that promised great growth. We focused on one of them. I asked, "How would you staff this opportunity?"

The manager of the department where this new task would fall said, "I think we could have two people. They will need to be skilled and trained, so we'd pay them about $65,000 a year."

I responded, "Very good, but let me ask this: what if you hired an exceptional new employee who could do the job of both people and you pay that person $100,000 a year? You'd save money on benefits and office expenses. Is that feasible?"

She thought for a minute, and then said, "Yes, in fact I know someone who would be perfect for this specialized, highly skilled role. A few months ago, I wouldn't have asked her to join our staff." People laughed. They knew exactly what she meant. "But now, I think she'd love it here... and she'd do a fantastic job!"

SUCCESS OR FAILURE

New expectations can be shaped out of success or failure, but in my experience, the motivation to change is far stronger in times of failure because people are desperate to find a way that works. When I met with the leadership team of the company, I didn't conduct an autopsy of the previous year or two. I didn't care how the patient died; I only cared how we could resurrect him! All the forensic analysis in the world wasn't going to breathe life back into the dead body of the company's culture, and it would have been a waste of time to try. But more than that, focusing on what had gone wrong had already produced a toxic mixture of blame and shame, discouragement and despair. We needed to put our attention on the future and bring as many people with us as possible. Hope, affirmation, and inspiration had been near zero, but the human heart thrives on these things. If we give people even a moderate amount of them, they stop shooting each other, they stop groveling in self-pity, and they find new, creative ways to make things work.

We might assume that a growing company or church has fewer tensions, but we'd be mistaken. Most leaders aren't satisfied with incremental growth. They look around at the needs of their communities and the stunning success of some pastors and business leaders, and they ask, "Why not us?" They put plans in gear to achieve a grand vision, but the pace of change can produce a host of unexpected difficulties.

> FOCUSING ON WHAT'S WRONG PRODUCES A TOXIC MIXTURE OF BLAME, SHAME, DISCOURAGEMENT, AND DESPAIR. THE HUMAN HEART THRIVES ON HOPE, AFFIRMATION, AND INSPIRATION.

SEVEN COMMON TENSIONS

My friend Ron Edmondson, the CEO of Leadership Network, has identified "7 Common Tensions You Can Expect During Fast Growth or Overwhelming Change." Too often, leaders are blindsided by these struggles because they assume *moving onward and upward* will be a smooth path. It isn't. I want to list these tensions and make some observations about them.

1. MISCOMMUNICATION

Some people don't get the memo...and some people don't read the memo. In times of rapid change, the leadership team can be so busy putting out fires and opening doors that they don't take time to close the loop on communication, which means following up to find out if the people who received the message understood it, have any questions, get answers, and give periodic feedback. Rapid growth invariably requires leaders to slow down long enough to communicate clearly.

2. CHANGING ROLES

Like the company I described in the opening story of this chapter, decline can cause changes in responsibilities, but so can growth. Leaders may discover that there has been a *sleeper* on the team, someone who has extraordinary talents that weren't being fully utilized, or the leaders may realize some people were at their limit of effectiveness when the organization was smaller. These people probably need to be moved to a role that better fits their capabilities.

3. POWER STRUGGLES

Squash them early and frequently. Don't let them fester and create distrust and resentment. Watch for people who call attention to their success and fail to give credit to others, and similarly, those who aren't excited about others' success. Look out for those who take responsibility without being assigned. This can be a wonderful trait of humility...or it can be a sign of power-seeking. When people have trouble collaborating and cooperating, it's often a sign that at least one of them insists on being in control. When I notice these tensions on a team, I don't let it run its course because that course is always destructive. When two people are jockeying for power, I call them in and speak into the situation, and I often assign them a task together to force them to collaborate and share power. If they can't work it out at that point, we then have a much bigger problem, and quite often, one of them needs to find new employment. Or perhaps both of them do.

4. BURNOUT

Rapid growth is exhilarating, but only for a while. After a period of time, the new level of effort becomes normalized; gradually, the ability to rebound each day and each week slips away. Chronic exhaustion, irritability, physical problems, sleeplessness, and weight problems are just a few of the symptoms of burnout. It's certainly a positive character trait to be eager and willing to shoulder the load, but all of us have limits. We need the courage to say, "No, I can't do that. I can handle this level of responsibility, but not that." We'd better not push people (or ourselves) so hard that they lose the joy of serving. Of course, there are times when we have to work harder than others, but we need to watch out that these times don't become our normal routine. Burnout isn't a badge of honor; it's a failure of leadership.

> **BURNOUT ISN'T A BADGE OF HONOR; IT'S A FAILURE OF LEADERSHIP.**

5. CONFUSION

Changing roles, new responsibilities, a different reporting structure, and added pressure can shake our confidence. It's perfectly fine to admit, "I don't know the answer to that." But chronic confusion may be a sign that someone is out of their depth.

6. COMPLACENCY

Times of extraordinary growth imply that our people are working very hard to achieve new levels of success, but ironically, a common reaction among at least a few is lethargy, distraction, and complacency. They're overwhelmed by the frenetic activity around them, and their defense is to withdraw and do less.

7. STRETCHED STRUCTURES

Many types of insects outgrow their shells, cast them off, and emerge with a bigger, stronger exoskeleton. In the same way, as organizations outgrow their systems and structures, they need to evaluate them, keep the ones that will work well in the next stage of growth, and change the ones that can't handle greater numbers. It's wise to anticipate the need for these changes before the tension produces big problems.[49]

Expansion of a company or a church always creates a measure of disruption. Wise leaders anticipate these tensions early in the planning stages so they can implement solutions all along the way.

ONBOARDING NEW HIRES

An important part of establishing new expectations in how we handle tension in our organizations is a fresh perspective of onboarding new hires. This isn't just an HR issue; it's a leadership issue. Far too often, we're only trying to fill a slot, to write a name on the organizational chart, to get a task accomplished. I believe we need to consider much more than this when we hire someone.

> **THINGS DON'T GO WRONG; THEY START WRONG. EMPLOYEES AND POTENTIAL HIRES NEED TO KNOW THE ORGANIZATION'S CULTURE AND VALUES.**

Why is it so important to give attention to onboarding? Because things don't *go* wrong; they *start* wrong. The process doesn't begin on the employee's first day, or even in the interview process. It starts in the boardroom as the corporate culture is shaped and imparted throughout the organization, and it can then be communicated on the company website so any interested person will see what the company values. In an article for *Inc.*, Peter Vanden Bos reports on his research about onboarding:

> Experts suggest you begin the orientation process before a candidate is formally hired by including ample information about your workplace and your culture in the Careers section on your website. "The orientation should begin at the first click of the

mouse when someone first goes on the company's website, so by the time the person comes in for the interview, they already know quite a lot about the organization," says Richard Jordan, a business coach who has been responsible for reshaping the recruiting and orientation process at a number of technology firms. That way, you are more likely to attract candidates who are more engaged with your company's goals and culture and are more likely to become highly productive employees.[50]

A powerful and clear onboarding process is a way to more carefully screen new hires, and if they're accepted on the team, it provides them with a smooth on-ramp so they can start well.

MODERN HEROES

ABRAHAM LINCOLN

We can look at a wide range of people in history who discovered how disruption can produce creativity. Abraham Lincoln grew up in the harsh home of his overbearing father, but his lack of education as a boy propelled him to study and become one of the foremost attorneys in his area. As the question of slavery became a dividing issue in the country, Lincoln took a stand, but not against slavery; his position was to stop the spread of slavery to the territories and new states. He ran for president as the candidate of the fledgling Republican Party. Three other men were arguably more qualified, but Lincoln won the nomination and the election. He surprised everyone by naming all three Republican competitors to his cabinet. He was willing to let strong men help him lead through the most turbulent era of our nation's history.

During the Civil War, Lincoln walked a number of tightropes. He wanted to keep the slave-owning border states in the Union, so he couldn't come out against slavery, but the abolitionists demanded the war be fought to free the slaves. The states loyal to the Union had far superior manpower and resources, but Lincoln's "generals were generally out-generaled" by the Southern commanders. Half the nation had seceded, and of the remaining half, half of them were Democrats who were zealously against him. With only about a fourth of the country on his side, Lincoln navigated the country to victory, suffering the grief of so many dead and wounded in battle while also dealing with the death of his beloved son, Willie, who suffered from typhoid fever, as well as the instability of his wife Mary. In her remarkable book, *Team of Rivals*, historian Doris Kearns Goodwin remarks:

> This, then, is a story of Lincoln's political genius revealed through his extraordinary array of personal qualities that enabled him to form friendships with men who had previously opposed him; to repair injured feelings that, left untended, might have escalated into permanent hostility; to assume responsibility for the failures of subordinates; to share credit with ease; and to learn from mistakes. He possessed an acute understanding of the sources of power inherent in the presidency, an unparalleled ability to keep his governing coalition intact, a tough-minded appreciation of the need to protect his presidential prerogatives, and a masterful sense of timing.[51]

And you think you've got it rough!

DIETRICH BONHOEFFER

Dietrich Bonhoeffer was a Lutheran scholar and theologian in Germany during the rise of Hitler and the Nazis in the 1930s. As a young man, he was a pacifist, but when he witnessed the anti-Semitic hatred of the Nazis, he joined a few other pastors to form the Confessing Church, which made a strong commitment to Christ at a time when many church leaders were mesmerized by Hitler's powerful rhetoric. As the Nazis consolidated power and began their systematic condemnation and elimination of the Jews, Bonhoeffer became a member of the German secret service—a double agent supposedly collecting information for the government, but actually conspiring to help Jews escape.

He accepted a teaching position at a seminary in America, but almost immediately, he changed his mind. He wrote a friend, "I have made a mistake in coming to America. I must live through this difficult period in our national history with the Christian people of Germany. I will have no right to participate in the reconstruction of Christian life in Germany after the war if I do not share the trials of this time with my people."

Bonhoeffer returned, taught in a seminary in the northern part of Germany, and participated in a plot to assassinate Hitler. The plot was discovered, and Bonhoeffer was arrested, tried, convicted, and imprisoned. His cheerfulness and strength of character impressed inmates and guards, and he continued to write beautiful and powerful letters about his commitment to Christ. One of them reads: "God lets himself be pushed out of the world on to the cross," he wrote. "He is weak and powerless in the world, and that is precisely the way, the only way, in which he is with us and helps us. [The Bible]...makes quite clear that Christ helps us, not by virtue of his omnipotence, but by virtue of his weakness and suffering.... The Bible directs man to God's powerlessness and suffering; only the suffering God can help."[52]

Dietrich Bonhoeffer was executed on April 9, 1945, one month before Germany surrendered. Because he rushed toward the tension instead of fleeing it, he became the spiritual leader of German believers during the war, and his impact is still powerful decades after his death.

MARY BARRA

Women in leadership roles experience an additional layer of tension. As they rise in their organizations, they face the invisible but very real *glass ceiling* that keeps them from the highest ranks...or at least makes it more difficult to get there.

In the man's world of auto manufacturing, Mary Barra rose to the top of General Motors as chairman of the board and CEO. She began working for the company as a co-op student in 1980, inspecting fenders and hoods as they rolled down the assembly line. After she graduated from college, she stayed at GM and rose steadily to become vice president of global manufacturing engineering, and then vice president of global product development—a role that is the most prestigious and the most pressurized in the company. In 2014, Barra became CEO, the first woman at the head of a major car company. In her first year, General Motors was forced to issue eighty-four recalls of over 30 million vehicles. She was summoned to testify before the United States Senate and received death threats over faulty ignition switches that were blamed for 124 fatalities.[53] But she weathered the storm and made a commitment to progress. She realized GM needed to become a leader in electric vehicles, so she pushed the company to come out with the Chevy Bolt EV, which arrived on the market before Tesla's first rollout of a car under $40,000.

The many recalls in her first year could have crushed Barra's spirit, but she didn't let them. Instead, she used the traumatic season to create new policies to encourage workers to report problems before cars arrive on the streets.

BRANCH RICKEY

Branch Rickey is one of the most remarkable people in the history of sports. You won't read about him in box scores. He didn't throw touchdown passes, didn't play cricket, and didn't compete with Michael Jordan in basketball. Rickey was the general manager of the Brooklyn Dodgers at a pivotal time in our nation's history. The owners had kept African-American players out of baseball for decades, but after World War II, the push for integration throughout the nation knocked on baseball's door. Still, the owners didn't answer.

Rickey was an innovator. When he arrived in Brooklyn, he set up batting cages and pitching machines, and he encouraged players to wear batting helmets. He kept a vast array of statistics and hired someone to analyze them and give him specific feedback during the season. All of these changes were innovative, the first of their kind in the game.

Innovation wasn't limited to equipment and statistics. Rickey was a Christian with strong convictions against the color barrier in baseball. Against the wishes of the rest of the team owners, he signed a Negro leagues star, Jackie Robinson, to a minor league contract right after

World War II. Robinson played for the Dodgers' minor league team in Montreal for a season, and he was so talented, Rickey brought him to the major league team. His first game was April 15, 1947. Everyone knew Robinson would receive verbal abuse from the racist fans. Rickey had prepared him by saying he was looking for a man who "had guts enough not to fight back."

It wasn't just the racists in the stands who heckled Robinson. Some of the players on the Dodgers refused at first to play with him. One of them, Bobby Bragan, bitterly opposed Rickey's decision to bring Robinson to the Dodgers. He tried to lead a revolt, joining with several other players threatening not to play if Robinson stepped on the field. The manager, Leo Durocher, told them Robinson was playing, and if they didn't want to play with him, they could leave the team. They stayed.

Robinson soon became a star on the field. He won the Rookie of the Year award and later was named Most Valuable Player in the league. His courage and skill opened the door for many other African Americans to play in the major leagues. It happened because one man, Branch Rickey, had a vision to give everyone the chance to play baseball. It was a commitment that was good for the sport and good for America, but Branch Rickey did it because it was simply the right thing to do.

Branch Rickey died in 1965. Many of the Dodgers, most of whom had retired years before, came to the funeral to pay their respects. A reporter asked Bobby Bragan why he had come. He said, "Because Branch Rickey made me a better man."

BENEFITS OF TENSION

I'm sure you know men and women whose lives are models to follow—and you've been thinking about them all through this book! They have faced significant struggles and the tensions that go with them, and they have learned to hold both sides in their hands at the same time.

Let me conclude by listing the benefits of developing the skill to embrace, resolve, and use tension.

WHAT YOU AVOID BY USING TENSION

First, here are some things you'll avoid. You'll realize the presence of tension isn't a flaw in you or a threat from others, so...

+ You won't be flustered or confused when you encounter tension.

+ You won't feel guilty that it's all your fault, and you won't assume it's all someone else's fault.

+ You'll experience less pressure to figure everything out and resolve it quickly and completely.

+ You won't be bullied when people demand their way.

+ You won't overlook people when they run away or hide.

+ You won't give in to the temptation to appease people instead of speaking the truth.

WHAT YOU GAIN BY USING TENSION

And on the positive side of the ledger, you'll realize...

+ Tension is essential for growth—yours and theirs.

+ Tension helps you think more deeply, engage more fully, wrestle with competing ideas and goals, and be genuine with others even when they disagree.

+ Tension makes you wiser and more approachable.

+ Tension gives you the opportunity to speak up, ask hard questions, listen, and take action.

In summary, tension is an inescapable reality. Embrace it. Resolve it when you can. Use it to help you and others grow. Let it make you a great leader.

Tension makes us better people.

THINK ABOUT IT:

1. What are some ways you've seen disruption lead to innovation?

2. When is it necessary to do an *autopsy* of a problem, and when is it a distraction?

3. Review the seven tensions you may experience during times of rapid growth. Which of these have you experienced? How did you respond?

4. What are some reasons we need to embrace tension in our spiritual lives? What happens when we're too rigid and drift toward extremes?

APPLY IT:

+ As you read this chapter, what tensions described here reminded you of your experiences?

+ How did you respond at the time?

+ How do you want to respond next time?

+ Who do you know who is experiencing a similar tension today?

+ How can you help this person embrace the tension, resolve the tension, or use the tension to stimulate an innovative solution?

ABOUT THE AUTHOR

Sam Chand's singular vision for his life is to *help others succeed*. A prolific author and renowned international business consultant, he develops leaders through consultations, Sam Chand Leadership Institute, Dream Releaser Coaching, and resources such as books, webinars, and digital downloads.

Sam consults with large churches and businesses on leadership and growth, conducts worldwide leadership conferences, and speaks regularly at corporations, business roundtables, seminars, and other leadership development opportunities.

Being raised in a pastor's home in India has uniquely equipped Sam to share his passion to mentor, develop, and inspire leaders to break all limits. He has been called a dream releaser, leadership architect, and change strategist.

In the 1970s, as a student at Beulah Heights College, Sam served as a janitor, cook, and dishwasher to finance his education. He returned in 1989 as president—and under his leadership, Beulah Heights University became the country's largest predominantly African-American Christian college.

Sam holds an honorary Doctor of Humane Letters from Beulah Heights University, an honorary Doctor of Divinity from Heritage Bible College, a Master of Arts in Biblical Counseling from Grace Theological Seminary, and a Bachelor of Arts in Biblical Education from Beulah Heights. He has mentored leaders in churches and ministries as well as international corporations and business start-ups. He was named one of the top thirty global leadership gurus by www.leadershipgurus.net.

Sam has authored more than a dozen books on leadership, including *The Sequence to Success: Three O's That Will Take You Anywhere in Life*; *New Thinking, New Future*; *Culture Catalyst*; *Bigger Faster Leadership*; *Who's Holding Your Ladder?*; *What's Shakin' Your Ladder?*; and *Leadership Pain*.

Sam and his wife, Brenda, have two adult daughters. They make their home in Atlanta, Georgia.

For more information or to connect with Sam, please visit
www.samchand.com

ENDNOTES

CHAPTER 1: TENSIONS IN YOUR PERSONAL LIFE

1. Richard Carlson and Benjamin Shield, *Handbook for the Soul* (New York: Back Bay Books 1995).

2. "The Evolving Definition of Work-Life Balance," Alan Kohll, *Forbes*, March 27, 2018 (www.forbes.com/sites/alankohll/2018/03/27/the-evolving-definition-of-work-life-balance/#7ff896989ed3).

3. "How Generation-Z Will Revolutionize the Workplace," Ashley Stahl, *Forbes*, September 10,

2019, (www.forbes.com/sites/ashleystahl/2019/09/10/
how-generation-z-will-revolutionize-the-workplace/#44bf113c4f53).

4. Stephen Covey, *The 7 Habits of Highly Effective People* (New York: Simon & Schuster, 2004), p. 165.

5. John Ortberg, *Overcoming Your Shadow Mission* (Grand Rapids: Zondervan, 2008), p. 12.

6. Theresa Bullard, Ph.D., "The Difference Between Success and Fulfillment," June 22, 2018 (www.theresabullard.com/single-post/2018/06/21/
The-Difference-Between-Success-and-Fulfillment).

CHAPTER 2: TENSIONS WITH PEOPLE

7. Mitch Albom, *Tuesdays with Morrie: An Old Man, a Young Man, and Life's Greatest Lesson* (New York: Broadway Books, 2017).

8. These recommendations have been curated from Chris Sonksen, www.churchboom.org.

9. Carla Rivera, "9 of the Biggest Social Media Influencers on Instagram," Digital Marketing Institute (digitalmarketinginstitute.com/en-us/
blog/9-of-the-biggest-social-media-influencers-on-instagram).

10. Ibid.

11. Cited by Judy Ford in *Wonderful Ways to Be a Family* (San Francisco: Red Wheel, 1998), p. 93.

12. Brené Brown, *Daring Greatly* (New York: Random House, 2012), p. 216.

13. Brian T. King, "How Good Leaders Handle Disagreement," June 26, 2018 (www.briantking.com/insights/
how-good-leaders-handle-disagreement-vs-weak-leaders).

CHAPTER 3: YOU CAN'T ESCAPE IT

14. Adapted from "Stress in Relationships: Their Sources and Antidotes," Susan Heitler, Ph.D., *Psychology Today*, May 30, 2013 (www.psychologytoday.com/us/blog/resolution-not-conflict/201305/stress-in-relationships-10-sources-and-their-antidotes).

15. Vocabulary.com.

16. Stuart Briscoe, "The Price of Progress," *Christianity Today*, Pastors, 1993 (www.christianitytoday.com/pastors/leadership-books/measuringup/mmpp01-8.html).

17. Lucy McGuire, "What is creative tension and how could it help you?," Virgin.com, May 15, 2018 (www.virgin.com/entrepreneur/what-creative-tension-and-how-could-it-help-you).

18. Robert M. Kaplan and Dennis P. Saccuzzo, *Psychological Testing* (Belmont, CA: Brooks/Cole Publishing Company, 1989), pp. 445-447.

19. "What Is Stress?" The American Institute of Stress (www.stress.org/daily-life).

CHAPTER 4: IT'S YOUR CHOICE

20. Jeff Wise, "How the Brave Are Different," *Psychology Today*, April 20, 2010 (www.psychologytoday.com/us/blog/extreme-fear/201004/how-the-bravest-are-different).

21. Dominic Dodd and Ken Favaro, "Managing the Right Tension," *Harvard Business Review*, December 2006 (hbr.org/2006/12/managing-the-right-tension).

CHAPTER 5: TENSIONS IN IMPLEMENTATION

22. Viktor E. Frankl, *Man's Search for Meaning* (Boston, MA: Beacon Press, 1992).

23. Jeff Haden, "The 8 Instinctive Habits of Remarkable Leaders," *Entrepreneur*, February 10, 2015 (www.entrepreneur.com/article/242713).

24. Ibid.

25. Sunny Bonnell, "4 Leaders Who Won by Following Their Instincts (Despite Being Told They Were Crazy)," *Inc.*, January 22, 2018 (www.inc.com/sunny-bonnell/how-to-follow-your-instincts-in-business-even-when-people-say-youre-crazy.html).

CHAPTER 6: TENSIONS WITH THE VISION

26. For more information and motivation, see "20 Reasons Why You Should Write Your Family History" by Carmen Nigro, New York Public Library, February 9, 2015 (www.nypl.org/blog/2015/02/09/reasons-to-write-your-family-history).

27. Adapted from a number of resources, including "Cycles of Failure and Cycles of Success and their Implications on Service Profit Chain" by John Dudovskiy, *Research Methodology*, November 27, 2012 research-methodology.net/cycles-of-failure-and-cycles-of-success-and-their-implications-on-service-profit-chain).

28. Lily Rothman, "What Happened to the Car Industry's Most Famous Flop?", *Time*, November 19, 2014 (time.com/3586398/ford-edsel-history).

29. Minda Zetlin, "5 Things the Smartest Leaders Know about Risk-Taking," *Inc.*, April 20, 2015 (www.inc.com/minda-zetlin/5-things-the-smartest-leaders-know-about-risk-taking.html).

30. Adam Hurley, "A Brief History of Bottled Water," *Kitchn*, February 23, 2016 (www.thekitchn.com/a-brief-history-of-bottled-water-228642).

31. Neil Petch, "The Five Stages of Your Business Lifecycle: Which Phase Are You In?" *Entrepreneur*, February 29, 2016 (www.entrepreneur.com/article/271290).

CHAPTER 7: TENSIONS WHEN FACING HARD CHOICES

32. Noam Wasserman, "The Founder's Dilemma," *Harvard Business Review*, February 2008 (hbr.org/2008/02/the-founders-dilemma).

33. "Teaching for Learning (XVI)," Martin M. Broadwell, February 20, 1969 (cited at edbatista.typepad.com/files/teaching-for-learning-martin-broadwell-1969-conscious-competence-model.pdf).

34. Paul R. Curtiss and Phillip W. Warren, *The Dynamics of Life Skills Coaching* (Training Research and Development Station: Prince Albert, Saskatchewan, 1973), p. 89.

35. For more on the dual role of pastor and CEO, look at my book, *Who's Holding Your Ladder* (New Kensington, PA: Whitaker House, 2016), pp. 34-38.

36. Tom Peters, *Excellence Now*, TomPeters! Blog (tompeters.com/quote/13381).

37. Robert Greenleaf, "The Servant as Leader," 1970 (www.greenleaf.org/what-is-servant-leadership).

CHAPTER 8: TENSIONS IN COMMUNICATION

38. Many organizations use the concept of cascading communication. For instance, see "Cascading Communication: Sending Out Your Message to the Entire Organization," Center for Management & Organizational Effectiveness (cmoe.com/blog/cascading-communication-sending-message-entire-organization).

39. Tiffany Mawhinney and Kimberly Betts, "Understanding Gen Z in the workplace," Deloitte (www2.deloitte.com/us/en/pages/consumer-business/articles/understanding-generation-z-in-the-workplace.html).

40. John Rampton, "Different Motivations for Different Generations of Workers: Boomers, Gen X, Millennials, and Gen Z," *Inc.*, October 17, 2017 (www.inc.com/john-rampton/different-motivations-for-different-generations-of-workers-boomers-gen-x-millennials-gen-z.html).

41. Stuart Briscoe, "The Price of Progress," *Christianity Today*, 1993, (www.christianitytoday.com/pastors/leadership-books/measuringup/mmpp01-8.html).

42. Megan Baker and Jelena Milutinovic, "The Importance of Face-to-Face Communication in the Digital Age," Australian Institute of Business, September 15, 2016 (www.aib.edu.au/blog/communication/face-to-face-communication-in-the-digital-age).

43. Daniel Threlfall, "Grow Your Church by Embracing Technology," *ShareFaith Magazine* (www.sharefaith.com/blog/2010/04/grow-church-embracing-technology).

CHAPTER 9: MANAGING TENSION (BEFORE IT MANAGES YOU!)

44. Dr. David G. Javitch, "7 Steps to Defuse Workplace Tension," *Entrepreneur*, July 29, 2010 (www.entrepreneur.com/article/207680).

45. Alan Kohll, "How to Build a Positive Company Culture," *Forbes*, August 14, 2018 (www.forbes.com/sites/alankohll/2018/08/14/how-to-build-a-positive-company-culture/#529b9fbb49b5).

46. Ibid.

47. See *Culture Catalyst* (New Kensington, PA: Whitaker House, 2018).

CHAPTER 10: NEW EXPECTATIONS, DIFFERENT RESULTS

48. Rick Warren, *Daily Inspiration for the Purpose Driven Life* (Grand Rapids, MI: Zondervan, 2003).

49. Adapted from "7 Common Tensions You Can Expect During Fast Growth or Overwhelming Change," Ron Edmondson, October 3, 2017 (ronedmondson.com/2017/10/7-tensions-you-can-expect-in-fast-growth.html).

50. Peter Vanden Bos, "How to Build an Onboarding Plan for a New Hire," *Inc.*, (www.inc.com/guides/2010/04/building-an-onboarding-plan.html).

51. Doris Kearns Goodwin, *Team of Rivals* (New York: Simon & Schuster: 2005), p. xvii.

52. Cited in "Dietrich Bonhoeffer: German theologian and resister," *Christianity Today* (www.christianitytoday.com/history/people/martyrs/dietrich-bonhoeffer.html).

53. David Shepardson, "GM compensation fund completes review with 124 deaths," *Detroit News*, August 24, 2015 (www.detroit-news.com/story/business/autos/general-motors/2015/08/24/gm-ignition-fund-completes-review/32287697).

GET FREE ACCESS TO MODULE ONE
OF THE *SAM CHAND LEADERSHIP INSTITUTE!*

The *Sam Chand Leadership Institute* is a virtual environment where high-performing leaders gather to create success, grow their network, and expand their capacity for more.

SAMCHANDLEADERSHIP.COM/SPECIAL

Welcome to Our House!

We Have a Special Gift for You

It is our privilege and pleasure to share in your love of Christian books. We are committed to bringing you authors and books that feed, challenge, and enrich your faith.

To show our appreciation, we invite you to sign up to receive a specially selected **Reader Appreciation Gift**, with our compliments. Just go to the Web address at the bottom of this page.

God bless you as you seek a deeper walk with Him!

WE HAVE A GIFT FOR YOU. VISIT:

whpub.me/nonfictionthx

WHITAKER
HOUSE